# Table of Contents

# How Does the Ketogenic Diet Work ?

Instead of counting calories and exercising six hours a day (who has that much free time?), the ketogenic diet takes a very different approach to weight loss, and it is backed by science.

Basically, when we eat food, particularly food that is high in carbohydrates, like bread or rice, the body converts the carbs into simple a sugar – glucose – and manufactures insulin, which is a hormone that pushes glucose from the bloodstream into the cells so that it can be used as energy.

Since glucose is used by the body as a primary source of energy, the fats that you also consume are not utilized; thus, they are stored in the liver and in fat cells called adipocytes. Moreover, if you consume more carbohydrates than the body needs, the excess glucose that is not used up is converted into glycogen and stored in the muscles and liver. If you don't use the glycogen, it is converted into fats; thus, you gain weight.

However, the human body has evolved over millions of years, and it has developed another form of energy source called ketones. In states of starvation or when the body cannot acquire carbohydrates for long periods, it turns to ketones or fats as a source of energy. The burning of ketones to fuel cellular activity is called ketosis. It is a process that has helped us survive over millions of years when food intake is minimal to none at all. Since the body cannot produce glucose from food, it metabolizes fat stored in the body; thus, you not only lose weight but also enjoy many other health benefits.

Once the ketones in the blood rise to a certain level, the body enters the state of ketosis. People enter the state of ketosis at different rates, but as a general rule, the body enters ketosis after three to four days of a low carbohydrate diet.

Ketosis happens when the liver starts breaking down fat into glycerol and fatty acids through a process called beta-oxidation. Instead of using energy from glucose, a body in ketosis fuels its cells using ketone bodies, thus essentially breaking down fats for fuel.   Optimal ketosis is achieved once the body stays in this state for at least two weeks, when the side effects diminish, and the benefits such as weight loss become more pronounced and evident.

## The Benefits of The Ketogenic Diet

The ketogenic diet is touted for its many health benefits. Aside from being used as a therapy for epilepsy, it comes with many other benefits. Below is a list of the benefits of following this particular diet.

### Weight Loss

Weight loss can be substantial if you follow the ketogenic diet. Several studies suggest that you can lose as much as 3% of your body weight in the first two days of following the diet. This is because the body burns stored fat that adds bulk to your total weight. Even more than burning off stored fat, what makes the ketogenic diet effective for weight loss is that it is filling; thus, it eliminates your cravings for sweet foods.

### Reduce the Risk of Type 2 Diabetes

People who have Type 2 diabetes suffer from insulin resistance. This means that they produce insulin, but the insulin does not work the way it should by pushing glucose into the cells. As a result, the amount of glucose in the bloodstream increases to high proportions. The ketogenic diet helps control and stabilize the release of insulin. When we eat carbs, insulin is released in relation to the elevated glucose level in the blood. Since the ketogenic diet eliminates carbohydrates from the diet, the body does not over-produce insulin.

## Reduce the Risk of Heart Disease

This diet has been shown to reduce the markers for heart diseases, such as triglycerides and cholesterol. Studies also show that this diet increases the level of HDL cholesterol – good cholesterol – in the blood.

## Protects Against Cancer

Some studies suggest that cancer cells feed on sugar in order to proliferate. Sugar is a highly processed and pro-inflammatory food that can increase the number of cancer cells in the body. The ketogenic diet has the ability to starve cancer cells because sugar and carbs are removed from the diet. Moreover, many of the foods in this diet are anti-inflammatory and rich in antioxidants that can fight off cancer cells.

## Fight Brain Diseases

Aside from epilepsy, the ketogenic diet is used to prevent other brain diseases. Studies show that cutting off glucose can reduce the risk of developing Alzheimer's disease. The brain uses ketones as an alternative source of energy, thus changing the cellular energy pathways that are not normally functioning in patients who are at risk of developing brain disorders. It can also increase mental performance as you don't experience big spikes in blood sugar; thus, you can have better focus and concentration.

## Increase Lifespan

Scientific evidence suggests that people who follow the ketogenic diet live longer than people who consume high amounts of carbohydrates. In fact, consumption of saturated fat from red meat is inversely associated with the development of stroke, which means that red meat has protective properties against stroke.

## Reduces Acne Breakout

People who suffer from acne breakouts can benefit from the ketogenic diet. Studies show that people who consume a high-carb diet develop more acne than those who consume a diet high in fat.

## Better Nutrition

Because there is no need for you to restrict calories, you are able to eat a lot of nutrient-dense, high-quality foods such as lean proteins, healthy fatty acids, and fiber from leafy vegetables. With this particular regimen, you don't develop a negative relationship with food. In fact, you will be able to make better food choices and ensure that you only consume foods that are healthy and beneficial for the body. It is better to focus on the types of food you consume than think about restricting your calorie intake. In a way, the ketogenic diet allows you to enjoy food as well as its many benefits.

# The Top 10 Ketogenic Diet Mistakes to Know about

We all make mistakes, including when following the ketogenic diet. While mistakes are costly, and this offsets our enjoyment of the benefits of this regimen, it is important to learn from these mistakes and move forward so that we can be successful in following this diet program. Here, then, are the top 10 ketogenic diet mistakes about which you need to know.

## Being Afraid of Fat

We have been taught that fat is bad and that it can kill us, but this is not the whole story. Remember that there are healthy and unhealthy fats. The ketogenic diet encourages you to consume healthy fats such as Omega-3s from deep-sea fish and Omega-6s from nuts. Our bodies thrive on healthy fats, and our livers have the ability break down fats into ketone bodies. So, the next time that someone tells you that fat is bad, think of the healthy fats instead!

## Not Taking Enough Salt

Many people believe that salt in the ketogenic diet is a recipe for high blood pressure and high-water retention. Well, that is true if you are a glucose burner. When the body burns glucose as the main source of energy, it requires a lot of water as well as stored glycogen, but once you achieve ketosis, ketones are much cleaner as burning fuel, and they don't require a lot of salt.

Thus, the body starts to remove excess water within a short period of time. Along with the removal of excess water is the release of sodium, magnesium, and potassium – all important micronutrients. This loss of electrolytes results in "keto flu" with symptoms of constipation, palpitations, fatigue, headaches, and light-headedness.

To avoid these side effects, increase your sodium intake to limit the loss of electrolytes from your body. When buying salt, you should opt for organic sea salt or Himalayan pink salt as they contain other minerals not found in manufactured table salt.

## Consuming Too Much Dairy

Dairy products such as hard cheeses, cream cheese, butter, and heavy cream are staples of the ketogenic diet. Unfortunately, not everyone can tolerate a lot of dairy products. As a result, some people suffer from inflammatory responses leading to weight gain.

Half the world's population has some intolerance to dairy, but they just don't know it. The intolerance to too much dairy elevates the production of the stress hormone cortisol that hurts your overall health. So, if you want to make the most out of your ketogenic diet, stay away from milk for at least a few weeks and see the difference.

## Not Having Enough Motivation

Why are you on a ketogenic diet? By now, you should be able to answer this question. If your main reason is to lose weight and look good, then you don't have enough reason to keep you going, and you are likely to give up once carb cravings set in.

You need to have the right mindset and motivation to keep you going with the ketogenic diet. It is not easy to give up all your favorite comfort foods, and the extent of your motivation will help you push through despite the ordeals that you face with this regimen. If you don't know how to have the right motivation, let these examples inspire you to keep going.

*I want to lose weight and get healthy because I want to live longer while still being able to do the things I love.*

*I have seen my loved ones suffer from the complications of diseases like diabetes.*

*I want to give up my addiction to carbs and sweet junk foods.*

*I want to be able to gain control over my body without my mind telling me what to constantly eat!*

*Alzheimer's disease runs in my family and I want to do something to avoid getting this disease.*

## Eating Too Much Protein

Remember that unlike other low-carb diets, the ketogenic diet stresses the importance of consuming more healthy fats. Just because there is minimal carb intake in this diet does not mean that you have to chow down on bacon and steaks. The body still has a way of producing glucose from proteins, called gluconeogenesis.

How can your body go into a state of ketosis if it is still producing glucose from fat? With the ketogenic diet, you need to consume more fat than protein. How do you know if you are in the state of ketosis? You can test your blood using ketone strips before and after high protein meals and with high-fat meals. Then compare.

## Snacking Too Much

Did you know that you should not eat too many times in a day? If you are following the ketogenic diet religiously, you will notice that you are eating fewer meals – snacks are no longer a necessity.

It's true that you do need to eat snacks if you are a glucose burner as glucose runs out too quickly, but fat as fuel is an entirely different thing. The body stores thousands or even millions of molecules of fat, and fat does not run out as easily as glucose, so you don't need to have a snack to replenish your energy.

However, if you are new to this diet, and snacking has been an integral part of your day, then you can continue to have some to ease into the transition as long as you choose your snack wisely in the form of nuts and seeds.

## Habitual Eating

The sad reality is that people don't eat because they are hungry. They eat out of habit. Humans are habitual creatures. We like to follow routines and do the same things at the same time every day. So, we have lunch at noon and supper at 6 p.m., and we tend to associate 3 p.m. with afternoon tea and dinner with TV.

These are habits and definitely not hunger signals. So, if you have to eat, eat because you are hungry and not because your watch is telling you what to do. The good news about habitual eating is that it can always be relearned with effort and patience.

## Not Getting Enough Sleep

Without enough sleep, the body is stressed and produces cortisol, which undermines weight loss. Moreover, once we don't get enough sleep, we tend to make poor choices by eating more to make up for the lack of sleep. So, get to bed early and make sure that you get at least six hours of sleep each night.

## Not Personalizing the Ketogenic Diet

Remember that what works for others might not work for you. The ketogenic diet is not a one-size-fits-all diet. It needs to be personalized to match your fitness levels. If you want to create the very best version of yourself with this diet, you have to be willing to experiment.

By answering certain questions such as how much protein is enough or too much; how much sleep do I need to effectively lose weight; do I have allergic reactions to ketogenic-approved foods like nuts or eggs; do I have dairy intolerance (and asking more!), you will create a ketogenic diet plan that works for you.

**Cheat Days**

Unlike other diet regimens, there are no cheat days with the ketogenic diet. So, don't tell yourself, "I lost a pound this week, so I deserve a reward." If you have this mindset, you are definitely set to fail. The problem with a cheat day is that it throws you out of ketosis, and you have to start again in order to achieve this state. Sure, you can start again, but remember that it takes about three to four days to achieve ketosis, so one cheat day is equivalent to three or four wasted days.

# Instant Pot Tricks and Tips

Using the Instant Pot is different from using conventional pressure cookers. Whatever you know about traditional pressure cookers is not applicable to the Instant Pot. Thus, it is crucial to know about the tips and tricks of using this kitchen appliance so you can optimize its use. Below are helpful tips, tricks, and practices on using your Instant Pot effectively.

## General Tips

Here are a few tips you need to know and follow in order to use your Instant Pot effectively and optimize the use of this nifty kitchen device.

- **Cook with at least ½ cup of water:** It is important to note that pressure is generated from steam; thus, you need at least ½ cup of water to generate steam that will, in turn, build the pressure within the inner pot.

- **Protect your counter from heat:** The heat generated by the Instant Pot can be so intense that your kitchen counter might get damaged.   So, if your working surface is not heat-proof, place a cutting board between the Instant Pot and the surface to protect it from heat damage.

- **Never delay the timer especially when cooking meats:** The feature of delay timer is very helpful especially if you want your meal to be ready by the time you get home.   However, if you are cooking meats, don't use the delay timer, as much as possible, because your meat might spoil after a few hours left at room temperature. If you really want to use the delay timer, make sure that you delay the timer for only a few minutes and never an hour.

- **If your recipe calls for stovetop cooking, reduce the cooking time with your Instant Pot:** If you are not using an Instant Pot cookbook to make your meals, you can still cook food perfectly if the recipe calls for conventional stovetop cooking. You simply reduce the cooking time indicated in the recipe to at least 1/3 as your pressure cooker cooks food faster than ordinary stovetop cooking.

## Cleaning Tips

To maintain the efficacy of your Instant Pot, it is crucial that you clean it after every use. Cleaning the Instant Pot is not difficult, but there are certain things that you need to be aware of so that you can clean this kitchen device properly.

- **Unplug from the power supply:** Before anything else, make sure the Instant Pot is unplugged from the power supply. When unplugging your Instant Pot from the power supply is also a good time to check there is no damage to the electrical cord.

- **Separate the lid, interior pot, and exterior body:** Separating all three components is very important as they require different cleaning methods. For the exterior housing, you can wipe it clean using a damp cloth. Make sure that you dry the housing with a dry kitchen towel afterward. Pay attention to the electrical wiring and circuit and don't wipe them with a damp towel so the electrical components are not damaged.

- **Thoroughly wash the interior pot:** The only washable component of the Instant Pot is the interior pot. Use warm soapy water to wash the interior pot and allow it to air dry or wipe it with a dry towel before placing it back in the exterior housing. Never place a wet interior pot in the housing as the moisture could damage the electrical components.

- **Take extra care in cleaning the lid:** The lid is made of washable and non-washable parts. Remove the washable parts, such as the floater valve and O-ring. Soak them in warm soapy water. For the other parts, carefully remove any stuck food particles. Completely wipe everything clean before re-assembling.

- **Do a "steam cleaning" at least once a week:** If you use your Instant Pot every day, make sure that you do a steam cleaning at least once a week. Steam cleaning removes any stuck food particles from the steam vent. To do this, pour one part vinegar and one part water in the inner pot and add a tablespoon of dishwashing soap. Close the lid and set the vent to "Sealing." Press the "Steam" button and adjust the time to five minutes. This will soften and dissolve the food particles in the steam vent.

# Instant Pot Do's and Don'ts

The Instant Pot is one of the most intuitive and revolutionary pressure cookers on the market. Aside from being efficient, this pressure cooker is touted as one of the safest and most efficient in the world. However, it is still important for you to understand how to use it properly so that you can optimize its use. So, below are the dos and don'ts of using the Instant Pot.

- **Use enough liquid when pressure cooking:** As mentioned earlier, the Instant Pot requires at least ½ cup of water to maintain enough pressure. Adjust the amount of liquid depending on the quantity of the ingredients that you use. For instance, ½ cup is adequate if you are cooking a few servings, but add more if you use more ingredients. The liquid does not need to come from water. It can be a combination of water, stock, and seasonings.

- **Do not fill it with too much liquid:** While using too little water is not good for pressure cooking because it does not generate enough pressure to cook food, using too much liquid is not good either. Fortunately, the Instant Pot has a *max line* that indicates how far you can fill the inner pot with water. On the other hand, if you are planning to cook food that expands substantially, such as grains or beans, use less of the ingredients so that there is more space for them to expand.

- **Never force open the lid:** It is important to note that the lid of the Instant Pot does not open if the pressure inside the inner pot is high. Before you open the lid, wait for the pressure to normalize. You can either do natural or quick pressure release.

- **When opening the lid, tilt away from you:** Even if you have released the pressure inside the Instant Pot, the environment inside the inner pot is still very hot.

So, when you open the lid, make sure that you tilt it away from you so that your hands or face don't get burned from the escaping steam.

- **Clean the Instant Pot after every use:**   Be sure to clean the Instant Pot every time you use it. This ensures that there are no food particles stuck in the steam release vent. Pay extra attention to the components of the lid, such as the O-ring or sealing gasket. Check for damage as the presence of nicks will make the Instant Pot unable to build up adequate pressure.

- **Never buy accessories and parts from third-party suppliers:** Let's say that you need to replace your sealing ring; make sure that you buy an authentic sealing ring (or other accessories for that matter) from the manufacturer and not from third-party suppliers. Accessories from third-party suppliers might not be compatible with your Instant Pot.

# Chapter 6: About the Recipes

Eating ketogenic-friendly meals does not mean that you are eating unappetizing food all the time! In fact, there are many delicious foods that will jumpstart your ketogenic journey. Remember that unlike other types of low-carb diets, the ketogenic diet focuses more on healthy fats than protein to trick the body into undergoing ketosis.

## Why five Ingredients

Many people love to cook but don't have time to prepare meals that contain a lengthy list of ingredients. Moreover, some people who want to eat healthily have novice kitchen skills, so a long recipe can be quite discouraging. So, below are the benefits of cooking recipes with five (5) ingredients or less.

- **Convenience:** A recipe with five ingredients or less is very convenient for many people. With only five ingredients, such recipes also require simple cooking methods.

- **Time savings:** People are always looking for ways to save time so they can deal with other more important things such as work. A 5-ingredient recipe gives them the impression that cooking is fun and easy.

- **Accessible ingredients:** In fact, a time-saving recipe should have no more than five ingredients. Commonly, the ingredients will be found in most pantries, so whipping up these dishes is very easy.

- **Less effort in the kitchen:** You don't need to break a sweat when preparing meals in the kitchen if you are using 5-ingredient recipes. In most cases, these recipes are one-pot meals, so you only need to combine everything, and you are good to go.

With 5-ingredient recipes, you have more time available to do what you love to do without sacrificing health, nutrition or tasty food.

## Notes About These Recipes

This book contains 100 great ketogenic-friendly recipes that you can try every day. The recipes included in this eBook are breakfast favorites; soups and stews; side dishes and snacks; seafood, poultry, pork, and beef dishes; desserts and sweet treats, as well as sauces and salad dressings.

Rest assured that you can utilize your Instant Pot with these recipes and that all the foods you cook will be not only simple to prepare but also delicious and healthy. With these recipes, you have a wide choice of foods that you can cook throughout the year and enjoy the benefits of the ketogenic diet for a long time.

## Notes on Ingredients

Writing a 5-ingredient cookbook can be tricky as the foods need to be not only ketogenic-friendly but also delicious. While there are many cookbooks available that use prepared and packaged ingredients, we believe that consuming only whole foods is the only way to go. Less is definitely more and using whole food ingredients brings out the natural flavors of the food as well as imparts more nutrition to the body.

# Breakfast Recipes

## Eggs with Avocado Buns

Serves:   1

Preparation Time: 5 minutes

Cooking Time: 5 minutes

### Ingredients

- 1 whole egg
- ½ red onion, sliced into rings
- 2 lettuce leaves, rinsed
- 1 ripe avocado, pitted and peeled
- ½ tablespoon sesame seeds

### Instructions

1. Place 1 cup of water in the Instant Pot.
2. Place the egg in the middle and close the lid.
3. Make sure that the steam release valve is set to "Sealing."
4. Press the "Manual" button and adjust the cooking time to 5 minutes.
5. Do quick pressure release.
6. Once the lid is open, peel the eggs. Slice the eggs and set aside.
7. Assemble the burger by place the egg slices, onion slices, and lettuce leaves in between the avocado slices.
8. Sprinkle with salt and pepper to taste.
9. Garnish with sesame seeds on top.

**Nutrition information:** Calories per serving: 478; Carbohydrates: 19.1g; Protein: 13.9g; Fat: 41.2g; Sugar: 0.1g; Sodium: 120mg; Fiber: 14g

# Spicy Cauliflower and Eggs "Skillet"

Serves:  4

Preparation Time: 5 minutes

Cooking Time: 7 minutes

## Ingredients

- 1 tablespoon olive oil
- 3 cloves of garlic, minced
- 1 head cauliflower, grated and squeezed dry
- 4 large eggs
- 4 jalapeno peppers, chopped

## Instructions

1. Press the "Sauté" button on the Instant Pot and heat the oil.
2. Stir in the garlic and sauté for 1 minute until fragrant.
3. Add the cauliflower and season with salt and pepper to taste.
4. Pour ½ cup of water and spread evenly on the bottom of the inner pot.
5. Make four wells in the cauliflower and gently crack an egg in each.
6. Sprinkle with jalapeno peppers.
7. Close the lid and make sure that the steam release valve is set to "Sealing."
8. Press the "Manual" button and adjust the cooking time to 6 minutes.

**Nutrition information:** Calories per serving:113; Carbohydrates: 6.2g; Protein: 4.6g; Fat: 9.5g; Sugar: 0g; Sodium: 30mg; Fiber: 4.8g

# Avocado and Salmon Breakfast

Serves:   1

Preparation Time: 10 minutes

Cooking Time: 10 minutes

## Ingredients

- 2 ounces wild salmon fillets
- Salt and pepper to taste
- 1 ripe avocado, pitted
- 2 tablespoons extra-virgin olive oil
- Juice of 1 lemon

## Instructions

1. Place a steamer basket inside the Instant Pot and add a cup of water.
2. Season the salmon fillets with salt and pepper to taste.
3. Place on top of the steamer basket.
4. Close the lid and set the steam release valve to "Sealing."
5. Press the "Steam" button and cook for 10 minutes until salmon is flaky.
6. Do quick pressure release.
7. Use fork to flake the salmon; place in a bowl.
8. Stir in olive oil and lemon juice.
9. Season with more salt and pepper to taste.
10. Spoon inside the hollow portion of the pitted avocado.

**Nutrition information:** Calories per serving: 661; Carbohydrates: 27.8g; Protein: 13.5g; Fat: 68.2g; Sugar: 0g; Sodium: 262mg; Fiber: 17.8g

# Instant Pot "Baked" Eggs with Greens

Serves:   8

Preparation Time: 5 minutes

Cooking Time: 4 hours

## Ingredients

- 8 large eggs
- ½ cup coconut milk
- ½ cup spinach, chopped
- ½ cup kale leaves, chopped
- ½ cup chard leaves, chopped

## Instructions

1. In a mixing bowl, mix the eggs and coconut milk. Season with salt and pepper to taste.
2. Stir in the rest of the ingredients.
3. Place the mixture in the Instant Pot.
4. Close the lid and make sure that the steam release valve is set to "Venting."
5. Press the "Slow Cooker" function and adjust the cooking time to 4 hours.

**Nutrition information:** Calories per serving: 91; Carbohydrates: 1.6g; Protein: 3.1g; Fat:8.4 g; Sugar: 0g; Sodium: 32mg; Fiber: 0.4g

# Slow-cooked Creamy Kale Eggs

Serves:   4

Preparation Time: 5 minutes

Cooking Time: 4 hours

## Ingredients

- 4 large eggs
- 1 tablespoon coconut oil
- 2 tablespoons chopped red bell peppers
- ½ cup coconut milk
- 1 cup kale leaves, chopped

## Instructions

1. Place the eggs, coconut oil, bell peppers, and coconut milk in a bowl and blend until well combined.
2. Season with salt and pepper. Stir once more.
3. Place the kale leaves in the inner pot and pour the egg mixture over the kale.
4. Close the lid and make sure that the steam release valve is set to "Venting."
5. Press the "Slow Cooker" function and adjust the cooking time to 4 hours.

**Nutrition information:** Calories per serving: 164; Carbohydrates: 4.7g; Protein: 4g; Fat: 15.5g; Sugar: 0g; Sodium: 16mg; Fiber: 2.3g

# Soft-Boiled Eggs on Avocado

Serves:　8

Preparation Time: 3 minutes

Cooking Time: 4 minutes

## Ingredients

- 8 eggs
- 4 small avocados, pitted
- Salt and pepper to taste

## Instructions

1. Place the eggs in the Instant Pot.
2. Add a cup of water.
3. Close the lid and set the steam release valve to "Sealing."
4. Press the "Steam" button and cook for 4 minutes.
5. Do quick pressure release.
6. Crack open the eggs onto the hollowed portion of the avocados.
7. Season with salt and pepper to taste.

**Nutrition information:** Calories per serving: 293; Carbohydrates: 10.2g; Protein: 11.9g; Fat: 25.8g; Sugar: 0.5g; Sodium: 110mg; Fiber: 6.8g

# Instant Pot Scrambled Eggs

Serves:   8

Preparation Time: 5 minutes

Cooking Time: 4 hours

## Ingredients

- 2 tablespoons olive oil
- 8 eggs, beaten
- ¼ cup coconut milk
- Salt and pepper to taste

## Instructions

1. Place all ingredients in a mixing bowl. Blend until well combined.
2. Pour into the Instant Pot.
3. Close the lid and make sure that the steam release valve is set to "Venting."
4. Press the "Slow Cooker" function and adjust the cooking time to 2 hours.
5. Open the lid and stir the eggs.
6. Close the lid and continue cooking for 2 more hours.

**Nutrition information:** Calories per serving: 179; Carbohydrates: 1.9g; Protein: 7.4g; Fat: 17.5g; Sugar: 0g; Sodium: 104mg; Fiber: 1.2g

# Ketogenic Basil Omelet

Serves:     6

Preparation Time: 5 minutes

Cooking Time: 4 hours

## Ingredients

- 2 tablespoons olive oil
- 6 eggs, beaten
- ¼ cup coconut milk
- Salt and pepper to taste
- 1 cup fresh basil leaves, chopped

## Instructions

1. In a mixing bowl, combine all ingredients except for the basil leaves.
2. Place the basil leaves in the inner pot.
3. Pour the egg mixture over the basil.
4. Close the lid and make sure that the steam release valve is set to "Venting."
5. Press the "Slow Cooker" function and adjust the cooking time to 4 hours.

**Nutrition information:** Calories per serving: 195; Carbohydrates: 2.3g; Protein: 9.4g; Fat: 16.5g; Sugar: 0g; Sodium: 104mg; Fiber: 1.8g

# Ketogenic Porridge

Serves: 1

Preparation Time: 5 minutes

Cooking Time: 4 hours

## Ingredients

- 2 eggs, beaten
- 1 tablespoon sesame seeds
- 5 tablespoons coconut cream, unsweetened
- 2 tablespoon coconut oil
- Salt to taste

## Instructions

1. In a mixing bowl, combine all ingredients.
2. Pour the egg mixture into the Instant Pot.
3. Close the lid and make sure that the steam release valve is set to "Venting."
4. Press the "Slow Cooker" function and adjust the cooking time to 4 hours.

**Nutrition information:** Calories per serving: 791; Carbohydrates: 7.9g; Protein: 22.9g; Fat: 77.5g; Sugar: 0g; Sodium: 211mg; Fiber: 3.7g

# Slow-cooked Spinach Omelet

Serves:   4

Preparation Time: 5 minutes

Cooking Time: 4 hours

## Ingredients

- 4 eggs, beaten
- 2 tablespoons olive oil
- Salt and pepper to taste
- 1 cup fresh spinach leaves, chopped
- 1 tablespoon fresh chives, chopped

## Instructions

1. In a mixing bowl, mix together the eggs, oil, salt, and pepper until well combined.
2. Place the spinach leaves in the Instant Pot and pour the egg mixture over the spinach.
3. Garnish with chopped chives.
4. Close the lid and make sure that the steam release valve is set to "Venting."
5. Press the "Slow Cooker" function and adjust the cooking time to 4 hours.

**Nutrition information:** Calories per serving: 205; Carbohydrates:3.7 g; Protein: 10.6g; Fat: 19.3g; Sugar: 0g; Sodium: 132mg; Fiber: 2.3g

# Ketogenic Western Omelet

Serves:   6

Preparation Time: 5 minutes

Cooking Time: 4 hours and 5 minutes

## Ingredients

- ½ cup ground beef
- 1 yellow onion, finely chopped
- ½ green bell pepper, seeded and finely chopped
- 6 eggs, beaten
- ¼ cup coconut milk

## Instructions

1. Place the ground beef in the Instant Pot and press the "Sauté" button.
2. Sauté for 5 minutes until lightly brown. Add the onion and bell pepper. Season with salt and pepper to taste.
3. Turn off the Instant Pot.
4. In a mixing bowl, mix the eggs and coconut milk until well combined.
5. Pour the mixture over the beef.
6. Close the lid and make sure that the steam release valve is set to "Venting."
7. Press the "Slow Cooker" function and adjust the cooking time to 4 hours.

**Nutrition information:** Calories per serving: 244; Carbohydrates: 2.7g; Protein: 10.6g; Fat: 20.5g; Sugar: 0g; Sodium: 124mg; Fiber: 1.7g

# Healthy Steamed Egg Muffin

Serves: 4

Preparation Time: 5 minutes

Cooking Time: 8 minutes

## Ingredients

- 1 tablespoon olive oil
- 4 strips of bacon, uncured
- 4 eggs, whole
- Salt and pepper to taste
- 4 slices of avocado

## Instructions

1. Place a steam rack in the Instant Pot and pour in a cup of water.
2. Grease 4 muffin cups with olive oil.
3. Place one strip of bacon in each muffin cup.
4. Crack an egg on top of each bacon strip.
5. Season with salt and pepper to taste.
6. Place the muffin cups on the steam rack.
7. Close the lid and make sure that the steam release valve is set to "Sealing."
8. Press the "Steam" function and adjust the cooking time to 8 minutes.
9. Do quick pressure release.
10. Garnish with avocado slices.

**Nutrition information:** Calories per serving: 501; Carbohydrates: 19.5g; Protein: 13.7g; Fat:43.9 g; Sugar: 0g; Sodium: 190mg; Fiber: 12.8g

# Fishermen's Eggs

Serves:  1

Preparation Time: 5 minutes

Cooking Time: 4 hours

## Ingredients

- 1 can organic sardines in olive oil
- ½ cup arugula leaves, shredded
- A dash of sage leaves
- Salt and pepper to taste
- 2 organic eggs, whole

## Instructions

1. Place the sardines in olive oil inside the Instant Pot.
2. Add the arugula leaves and sage. Season with salt and pepper to taste.
3. Make 2 wells in the sardine mixture and crack open an egg into each well.
4. Close the lid and make sure that the steam release valve is set to "Venting."
5. Press the "Slow Cooker" function and adjust the cooking time to 4 hours.

**Nutrition information:** Calories per serving: 456; Carbohydrates: 5.2g; Protein: 25.6g; Fat: 48.9g; Sugar: 0g; Sodium: 588mg; Fiber: 3.5g

# Blackberry Egg Cake

Serves:   3

Preparation Time: 10 minutes

Cooking Time: 8 minutes

## Ingredients

- 5 large eggs
- 1 tablespoon coconut oil
- 3 tablespoon coconut flour
- ½ cup fresh blackberries
- Zest from ½ an orange

## Instructions

1. Place a steam rack in the Instant Pot and pour in a cup of water.
2. In a mixing bowl, combine the eggs, coconut oil, and coconut flour until well combined. Season with a pinch of salt.
3. Add the blackberries and orange zest.
4. Pour into muffin cups.
5. Place the muffin cups on the steam rack.
6. Close the lid and make sure that the steam release valve is set to "Sealing."
7. Press the "Steam" function and adjust the cooking time to 8 minutes.
8. Do quick pressure release.

**Nutrition information:** Calories per serving: 172; Carbohydrates: 11.4g; Protein: 5.6g; Fat: 16.9g; Sugar: 0g; Sodium: 31mg; Fiber: 8.9g

# Eggs with Avocados

Serves: 4

Preparation Time: 10 minutes

Cooking Time: 6 minutes

## Ingredients

- 6 eggs, whole
- 1 large avocado, peeled and mashed
- 1 tablespoon lemon juice
- 1 teaspoon minced garlic
- 1 teaspoon paprika

## Instructions

1. Place the eggs in the Instant Pot and add a cup of water.
2. Close the lid and make sure that the steam release valve is set to "Sealing."
3. Press the "Manual" button and adjust the cooking time to 6 minutes.
4. Do quick pressure release.
5. Allow the eggs to cool in iced water.
6. Crack and peel the eggs.
7. Mash the eggs in a mixing bowl.
8. Stir in the avocado, lemon juice, and garlic.
9. Season with salt and pepper to taste.
10. Mix to combine.
11. Sprinkle with paprika.

**Nutrition information:** Calories per serving: 278; Carbohydrates: 6.6g; Protein: 12.1g; Fat: 21.9g; Sugar: 0.4g; Sodium: 157mg; Fiber: 2.9g

# Scrambled Eggs with Smoked Salmon

Serves:  3

Preparation Time: 5 minutes

Cooking Time: 4 hours

## Ingredients

- 6 large eggs, beaten
- 3 ounces wild smoked salmon, flaked
- 1 tablespoon shallots
- 1 tablespoon capers
- Salt and pepper to taste

## Instructions

1. Place all ingredients in a mixing bowl and blend until well combined.
2. Pour into the Instant Pot.
3. Close the lid and make sure that the steam release valve is set to "Venting."
4. Press the "Slow Cooker" function and adjust the cooking time to 4 hours.

**Nutrition information:** Calories per serving: 170; Carbohydrates: 3.4g; Protein: 9.3g; Fat: 14.2g; Sugar: 0.2g; Sodium: 101mg; Fiber:2.1g

# Soups and Stews

## Turmeric Chicken Soup

Serves:  3

Preparation Time: 5 minutes

Cooking Time: 15 minutes

### Ingredients

- 2½ teaspoons turmeric powder
- 3 chicken breasts with skin, boneless
- 4 cups water
- 1 bay leaf
- ½ cup coconut milk

### Instructions

1. Place all ingredients in the Instant Pot.
2. Give a good stir to mix everything.
3. Close the lid and make sure that the vent points to "Sealing."
4. Press the "Poultry" button and adjust the time to 15 minutes.
5. Do natural pressure release.

**Nutrition information:** Calories per serving: 599; Carbohydrates: 3.8g; Protein: 46.8g; Fat: 61.4g; Sugar: 0g; Sodium: 196mg; Fiber: 1.4g

# Egg Drop Soup with Shredded Chicken

Serves:   6

Preparation Time: 5 minutes

Cooking Time: 15 minutes

## Ingredients

- 2 tablespoons coconut oil
- 1 onion, minced
- 1 celery, chopped
- 3 cups shredded chicken
- 4 cups water
- 4 eggs, beaten

## Instructions

1. Press the "Sauté" button on the Instant Pot and heat the oil.
2. Sauté the onion and celery for 2 minutes or until fragrant.
3. Add the chicken and water.
4. Season with salt and pepper to taste.
1. Close the lid and make sure that the vent points to "Sealing."
6. Press the "Poultry" button and adjust the time to 10 minutes.
5. Do natural pressure release.
6. Once the lid is open, press the "Sauté" button and allow the soup to simmer.
7. Very gently, gradually pour in the beaten eggs and allow to simmer for 3 more minutes.

**Nutrition information:** Calories per serving: 154; Carbohydrates: 2.9g; Protein: 9.6g; Fat: 12.8g; Sugar: 0g; Sodium: 482mg; Fiber: 1.4g

# Asian Egg Drop Soup

Serves:   3

Preparation Time: 5 minutes

Cooking Time: 9 minutes

## Ingredients

- 3 cups water
- 3 tablespoon coconut oil
- 2 cups kale, chopped
- 1 teaspoon grated ginger
- 2 eggs, beaten

## Instructions

1. Place all ingredients except for the beaten eggs in the Instant Pot. Season with salt and pepper to taste.
2. Close the lid and make sure that the vent points to "Sealing."
3. Press the "Manual" button and adjust the time to 6 minutes.
4. Do natural pressure release.
5. Once the lid is open, press the "Sauté" button and allow the soup to simmer.
6. Very gently, gradually pour in the beaten eggs and allow to simmer for 3 more minutes.

**Nutrition information:** Calories per serving: 209; Carbohydrates: 1.7g; Protein: 6.5g; Fat: 20.3g; Sugar:0g; Sodium: 77mg; Fiber: 0.7g

# Leek and Salmon Soup

Serves:   4

Preparation Time: 5 minutes

Cooking Time: 10 minutes

## Ingredients

- 2 tablespoons avocado oil
- 4 leeks, trimmed and chopped
- 3 cloves of garlic, minced
- 1 ¾ cup coconut milk
- 1 pound salmon, sliced into bite-sized pieces

## Instructions

1. Place all ingredients in the Instant Pot. Season with salt and pepper to taste.
2. Stir to combine all ingredients.
3. Close the lid and make sure that the vent points to "Sealing."
4. Press the "Manual" button and adjust the time to 10 minutes.

**Nutrition information:** Calories per serving: 535; Carbohydrates: 19.5g; Protein:27.3g; Fat: 40.9g; Sugar: 2g; Sodium: 545mg; Fiber: 10.5g

# Thai Coconut Soup

Serves:   2

Preparation Time: 5 minutes

Cooking Time: 6 minutes

## Ingredients

- 2 cups water
- 1 ½ cups organic coconut milk
- 3 kaffir limes
- 6 ounces shrimps
- 1 cup fresh cilantro

## Instructions

1. Place all ingredients, except for the cilantro, in the Instant Pot.
2. Close the lid and make sure that the vent points to "Sealing."
3. Press the "Manual" button and adjust the time to 6 minutes.
4. Do natural pressure release.
5. Once the lid is open, garnish with the fresh cilantro.

**Nutrition information:** Calories per serving: 517; Carbohydrates: 15.4g; Protein: 21.9g; Fat: 44.6g; Sugar: 2g; Sodium: 777mg; Fiber: 7.3g

# Ginger Halibut Soup

Serves:  4

Preparation Time: 5 minutes

Cooking Time: 12 minutes

## Ingredients

- 2 tablespoons coconut oil
- 1 large onion, chopped
- 2 cups water
- 1 pound halibut, cut into chunks
- 2 tablespoons minced fresh ginger

## Instructions

1. Press the "Sauté" button on the Instant Pot and heat the oil.
2. Sauté the onion until fragrant.
3. Pour in the water and the rest of the ingredients. Season with salt and pepper to taste.
4. Close the lid and make sure that the vent points to "Sealing."
5. Press the "Manual" button and adjust the time to 10 minutes.

**Nutrition information:** Calories per serving: 259; Carbohydrates: 7.9g; Protein: 10.9g; Fat: 22.8g; Sugar: 0.8g; Sodium: 388mg; Fiber: 4.3g

# Salmon Head Soup

Serves:   1

Preparation Time: 5 minutes

Cooking Time: 12 minutes

## Ingredients

- 4 tablespoons coconut oil
- 1 onion, sliced
- 3 cups water
- 1 salmon head
- 1 3-inch piece of ginger, slivered

## Instructions

1. Press the "Sauté" button on the Instant Pot and heat the oil.
2. Sauté the onion until fragrant.
3. Pour in the water and add the salmon head and ginger.
4. Season with salt and pepper to taste.
5. Close the lid and make sure that the vent points to "Sealing."
6. Press the "Manual" button and adjust the time to 10 minutes.
7. Do quick pressure release.

**Nutrition information:** Calories per serving: 474; Carbohydrates: 1.8g; Protein: 15.3g; Fat: 54.4g; Sugar: 0g; Sodium: 115mg; Fiber: 0g

# Salmon Stew

Serves:   3

Preparation Time: 5 minutes

Cooking Time:13 minutes

## Ingredients

- 3 tablespoons olive oil
- 3 cloves of garlic, minced
- 3 cups water
- 6 8-ounce salmon fillets
- 3 cups spinach leaves

## Instructions

1. Press the "Sauté" button on the Instant Pot and heat the olive oil.
2. Sauté the garlic until fragrant.
3. Add the water and salmon fillets. Season with salt and pepper to taste.
4. Close the lid and make sure that the vent points to "Sealing."
5. Press the "Manual" button and adjust the time to 10 minutes.
6. Do quick pressure release.
7. Once the lid is open, press the "Sauté" button and add the spinach.
8. Allow to simmer for 3 minutes.

**Nutrition information:** Calories per serving: 825; Carbohydrates: 2.1g; Protein: 46.1g; Fat: 94.5g; Sugar: 0g; Sodium: 1993mg; Fiber: 0.8g

# Coconut Seafood Soup

Serves: 5

Preparation Time: 5 minutes

Cooking Time: 8 minutes

## Ingredients

- 2 cups water
- 1 thumb-size ginger, crushed
- 4 tilapia fillets
- 10 shrimps, peeled and deveined
- 1 cup coconut milk

## Instructions

1. Place all ingredients in the Instant Pot.
2. Season with salt and pepper to taste, then give a good stir.
3. Close the lid and make sure that the vent points to "Sealing."
4. Press the "Manual" button and adjust the time to 8 minutes.

**Nutrition information:** Calories per serving: 238; Carbohydrates: 2.7; Protein: 13.6g; Fat: 28.8g; Sugar: 0g; Sodium: 111mg; Fiber: 1.7g

# Poached Egg Soup

Serves:    2

Preparation Time: 5 minutes

Cooking Time: 36 minutes

## Ingredients

- 2 cups water
- 1 pound chicken bones
- 2 eggs, whole
- 1 head romaine lettuce, chopped
- Salt and pepper to taste

## Instructions

1. Place the water and chicken bones in the Instant Pot.
2. Close the lid and make sure that the vent points to "Sealing."
3. Press the "Poultry" button and adjust the time to 30 minutes.
4. Do quick pressure release.
5. Take the bones out and discard.
6. Press the "Sauté" button and allow the soup to simmer.
7. Once simmered, carefully crack the eggs open and stir for 3 minutes.
8. Add the lettuce and season with salt and pepper.
9. Allow to simmer for 3 more minutes.

**Nutrition information:** Calories per serving: 443; Carbohydrates: 4.3g; Protein: 58.3g; Fat: 39.2g; Sugar: 0g; Sodium: 316mg; Fiber: 2.1g

# Simple Chicken and Kale Soup

Serves:    4

Preparation Time: 5 minutes

Cooking Time: 20 minutes

## Ingredients

- 3 tablespoons coconut oil
- 1 onion, diced
- 2 celery stalks, chopped
- 1 pound chicken breasts, skin on and bone removed
- 4 cups kale, chopped

## Instructions

1. Press the "Sauté" button on the Instant Pot and heat the oil.
2. Sauté the onions and celery until fragrant.
3. Add the chicken breasts and sear for 2 minutes on each side.
4. Pour in 3 cups water and season with salt and pepper to taste.
5. Close the lid and make sure that the vent points to "Sealing."
6. Press the "Poultry" button and adjust the time to 15 minutes.
7. Do natural pressure release and open the lid.
8. Once the lid is open, press the "Sauté" button and add the kale.
9. Allow to simmer for 3 minutes.

**Nutrition information:** Calories per serving: 303; Carbohydrates: 2.2g; Protein: 20.8g; Fat: 29.3g; Sugar: 0g; Sodium: 85mg; Fiber: 1.4g

# Leftover Shredded Chicken Soup

Serves:   3

Preparation Time: 5 minutes

Cooking Time: 12 minutes

## Ingredients

- 2 tablespoons coconut oil
- 1 onion, chopped
- 8 cloves of garlic, minced
- 2 cups leftover chicken meat, shredded
- 7 cups water

## Instructions

1. Press the "Sauté" button on the Instant Pot and heat the oil.
2. Sauté the onions and garlic until fragrant.
3. Add the chicken meat and season with salt and pepper to taste.
4. Pour in the water. Season with more salt and pepper.
5. Close the lid and make sure that the vent points to "Sealing."
6. Press the "Manual" button and adjust the time to 10 minutes.

**Nutrition information:** Calories per serving: 356; Carbohydrates: 2.5g; Protein:23.4 g; Fat: 32.1g; Sugar: 0g; Sodium: 808mg; Fiber: 1.6g

# Cream of Broccoli Soup

Serves:     5

Preparation Time: 5 minutes

Cooking Time: 34 minutes

## Ingredients

- ½ pound chicken bones
- 4 cups water
- 2 broccoli heads, cut into florets
- 1 small avocado, sliced
- 1 teaspoon paprika powder

## Instructions

1. Place the chicken bones and water in the Instant Pot.
2. Season with salt and pepper to taste
3. Close the lid and make sure that the vent points to "Sealing."
4. Press the "Manual" button and adjust the time to 30 minutes.
5. Do quick pressure release.
6. Once the lid is open, discard the bones.
7. Stir in the broccoli.
8. Close the lid again and press the "Manual" button and cook for 4 minutes.
9. Do quick pressure release.
10. Transfer all contents into a blender. Add the avocado slices.
11. Pulse until smooth.
12. Place in a bowl and sprinkle with paprika powder.

**Nutrition information:** Calories per serving: 118; Carbohydrates: 1.9g; Protein: 7.3; Fat: 10.3g; Sugar: 0g; Sodium: 43 mg; Fiber: 0.5g

# Turkey with Ginger and Turmeric Soup

Serves:   4

Preparation Time: 5 minutes

Cooking Time: 17 minutes

## Ingredients

- 3 tablespoons coconut oil
- 2 stalks of celery, chopped
- 1 thumb-size ginger, sliced
- 1 teaspoon turmeric powder
- 1 pound turkey meat, chopped into bite-sized pieces

## Instructions

1. Press the "Sauté" button on the Instant Pot and heat the oil.
2. Stir in the celery, ginger, and turmeric powder until fragrant.
3. Add the turkey meat and stir for another minute.
4. Pour in 3 cups of water and season with salt and pepper to taste.
5. Close the lid and make sure that the vent points to "Sealing."
6. Press the "Manual" button and adjust the time to 15 minutes.
7. Do natural pressure release.

**Nutrition information:** Calories per serving: 287; Carbohydrates: 0.8g; Protein: 22.8g; Fat: 24.3g; Sugar: 0g; Sodium: 82mg; Fiber:0g

# Slow-cooked Cabbage and Chuck Roast Stew

Serves: 10

Preparation Time: 5 minutes

Cooking Time: 36 minutes

## Ingredients

- 3 tablespoons olive oil
- 2 onions, cut into wedge
- 1 clove of garlic, minced
- 3 pounds chuck roast, cut into chunks
- 1 small head of cabbage, cut into wedges

## Instructions

1. Press the "Sauté" button on the Instant Pot and heat the oil.
2. Sauté the onions and garlic until fragrant.
3. Add the chuck roast and stir for 3 minutes.
4. Pour in 6 cups of water and season with salt and pepper to taste.
5. Close the lid and make sure that the vent points to "Sealing."
6. Press the "Manual" button and adjust the time to 30 minutes.
7. Do natural pressure release.
8. Once the lid is open, press the "Sauté" button and add the cabbage.
9. Allow to simmer for 3 minutes.

**Nutrition information:** Calories per serving: 312; Carbohydrates: 6.3g; Protein: 20.3g; Fat: 15.6g

# Thai Tom Saap Pork Ribs Soup

Serves:    4

Preparation Time: 5 minutes

Cooking Time: 40 minutes

## Ingredients

- 1 pound pork spare ribs
- 4 lemongrass stalks
- 10 slices galangal
- 10 kaffir lime leaves
- 3 tablespoons sesame oil

## Instructions

1. In the Instant Pot, place the spare ribs, lemon grass, galangal, and kaffir lime leaves.
2. Pour in 6 cups of water and season with salt and pepper to taste.
3. Close the lid and make sure that the vent points to "Sealing."
4. Press the "Manual" button and adjust the time to 40 minutes.
5. Do natural pressure release.
6. Once the lid is open, pour in sesame oil and garnish with cilantro if desired.

**Nutrition information:** Calories per serving: 281; Carbohydrates: 2.2g; Protein: 19.9g; Fat: 26.9g; Sugar: 0g; Sodium: 107mg; Fiber: 0g

# Side Dish and Snacks

## Mashed Cauliflower

Serves:   3

Preparation Time: 10 minutes

Cooking Time: 7 minutes

### Ingredients

- 1 cauliflower head, chopped into florets
- ½ cup grass-fed butter
- 2 tablespoons olive oil
- Juice of ½ lemon, freshly squeezed
- Salt and pepper to taste

### Instructions

1. Place a steam rack in the Instant Pot and add a cup of water.
2. Place the cauliflower florets on the steam rack.
3. Close the lid and make sure that the vent points to "Sealing."
4. Press the "Steam" button and adjust the time to 7 minutes.
5. Do quick pressure release.
6. Place the cauliflower in a food processor and add the rest of the ingredients.
7. Pulse until smooth.

**Nutrition information:** Calories per serving: 41; Carbohydrates: 2.4g; Protein: 0.7g; Fat: 4.9g; Sugar:0g; Sodium: 23mg; Fiber: 1.7g

# Slow-cooked Brussels Sprouts

Serves: 4

Preparation Time: 5 minutes

Cooking Time: 4 hours

## Ingredients

- 1 pound uncured bacon slices, fried and crumbled
- 2 pounds Brussels sprouts
- 3 tablespoons ghee
- 1 teaspoon garlic powder
- ¼ teaspoon salt

## Instructions

1. Place all ingredients in the Instant Pot.
2. Close the lid and make sure that the vent points to "Venting."
3. Press the "Slow Cooker" button and adjust the time to 4 hours.
4. Halfway through the cooking time, open the lid and stir the Brussels sprouts.

**Nutrition information:** Calories per serving: 528; Carbohydrates: 28.1g; Protein: 20g; Fat: 42.8g; Sugar: 0.4g; Sodium: 1932mg; Fiber: 11.9g

# Cauliflower Fried Rice

Serves:   5

Preparation Time: 10 minutes

Cooking Time: 10 minutes

## Ingredients

- 1 head cauliflower, halved
- 2 tablespoons sesame oil
- 2 onions, chopped
- 1 egg, beaten
- 5 tablespoons coconut aminos

## Instructions

1. Place a steam rack in the Instant Pot and add a cup of water.
2. Place the cauliflower florets on the steam rack.
3. Close the lid and make sure that the vent points to "Sealing."
4. Press the "Steam" button and adjust the time to 7 minutes.
5. Do quick pressure release.
6. Clean the Instant Pot for later.
7. Place the cauliflower florets in a food processor and pulse until grainy in texture.
8. Press the "Sauté" button on the Instant Pot and heat the oil.
9. Stir in the onions until fragrant.
10. Stir in the egg and break up into small pieces.
11. Add the cauliflower rice and season with coconut aminos.
12. Adjust the seasoning with more salt and pepper to taste.

**Nutrition information:** Calories per serving: 108; Carbohydrates: 4.3g; Protein: 3.4g; Fat: 8.2g; Sugar: 0g; Sodium: 126mg; Fiber: 2.5g

# Avocado Deviled Eggs

Serves:    6

Preparation Time: 10 minutes

Cooking Time: 6 minutes

## Ingredients

- 6 eggs
- 1 avocado, pitted and meat scooped out
- ¼ teaspoon garlic powder
- ¼ teaspoon smoked paprika
- 3 tablespoons chopped cilantro

## Instructions

1. Place the eggs in the Instant Pot and add 1½ cups of water.
2. Close the lid and make sure that the vent points to "Sealing."
3. Press the "Manual" button and adjust the time to 6 minutes.
4. Do quick pressure release.
5. Allow the eggs to completely cool before cracking and peeling off the shells.
6. Slice the eggs lengthwise and scoop out the yolk.
7. Place the yolk in a mixing bowl and add the avocado, garlic powder, and paprika. Season with salt and pepper to taste. Mix until well combined.
8. Fill the hollows of the egg whites with the avocado-yolk mixture.
9. Garnish with cilantro.

**Nutrition information:** Calories per serving: 184; Carbohydrates: 4.1g; Protein: 9.6g; Fat: 14.5g; Sugar: 0g; Sodium: 102mg; Fiber: 3.5g

# Crustless Spinach Quiche Bites

Serves:     12

Preparation Time: 5 minutes

Cooking Time: 4 hours

## Ingredients

- 2 tablespoons coconut oil
- 1 onion, chopped
- 2 cups chopped spinach
- 8 eggs, beaten
- Salt and pepper to taste

## Instructions

1. Press the "Sauté" button on the Instant Pot and heat the oil.
2. Sauté the onion until fragrant.
3. Stir in the spinach and wilt for one minute.
4. Pour in the eggs and season with salt and pepper to taste.
5. Close the lid and make sure that the vent points to "Venting."
6. Press the "Slow Cook" button and adjust the time to 4 hours.
7. Allow to cool.
8. When serving, slice the quiche into bite-sized pieces.

**Nutrition information:** Calories per serving: 112; Carbohydrates: 2.1g; Protein: 6.3g; Fat: 9.7g; Sugar: 0g; Sodium: 73mg; Fiber: 1.4g

# Creamed Kale with Mushrooms

Serves:   3

Preparation Time: 5 minutes

Cooking Time: 8 minutes

## Ingredients

- 3 tablespoons coconut oil
- 3 cloves of garlic, minced
- 1 bunch kale, stems removed, and leaves chopped
- 5 cremini mushrooms, sliced
- ¾ cup coconut milk

## Instructions

1. Press the "Sauté" button on the Instant Pot and heat the oil.
2. Sauté the garlic until fragrant. Add the rest of the ingredients.
3. Season with salt and pepper to taste.
4. Close the lid and make sure that the vent points to "Sealing."
5. Press the "Manual" button and adjust the time to 6 minutes.
6. Do quick pressure release.

**Nutrition information:** Calories per serving: 288; Carbohydrates: 10.8g; Protein: 3.1g; Fat: 28.1g; Sugar: 0g; Sodium: 19mg; Fiber: 6.2g

# Slow-cooked Asparagus Side Dish

Serves:   3

Preparation Time: 5 minutes

Cooking Time: 2 hours

## Ingredients

- 12 asparagus spears, trimmed
- 2 tablespoons olive oil
- 2 cloves of garlic, minced
- ¼ teaspoon paprika
- Salt and pepper to taste

## Instructions

1. Place all ingredients in the Instant Pot.
2. Give a good stir.
3. Close the lid and make sure that the vent points to "Venting."
4. Press the "Slow Cook" button and adjust the time to 2 hours.

**Nutrition information:** Calories per serving: 92; Carbohydrates: 2.7g; Protein: 0.7g; Fat: 9.1g; Sugar: 0g; Sodium: 24mg; Fiber: 1.3g

# Chinese Eggplant In "Soy" Sauce

Serves:  2

Preparation Time: 5 minutes

Cooking Time: 5 hours

## Ingredients

- 2 eggplants, sliced into 3-inch in length
- ¼ cup coconut aminos
- 1 teaspoon grated ginger
- 3 cloves of garlic, minced
- 4 tablespoons coconut oil

## Instructions

1. Place all ingredients in the Instant Pot.
2. Season with salt and pepper to taste and adjust the liquid by adding water if necessary.
3. Give a good stir.
4. Close the lid and make sure that the vent points to "Venting."
5. Press the "Slow Cook" button and adjust the time to 5 hours.

**Nutrition information:** Calories per serving: 385; Carbohydrates: 35g; Protein: 5.8g; Fat: 28.3g; Sugar: 0g; Sodium: 48mg; Fiber: 20.9g

# Boiled Peanuts

Serves:  8

Preparation Time: 5 minutes

Cooking Time: 10 minutes

## Ingredients

- ½ pounds peanuts, unsalted
- 1½ cups water
- ½ tablespoon salt

## Instructions

1. Place everything in the Instant Pot.
2. Close the lid and make sure that the vent points to "Sealing."
3. Press the "Manual" button and adjust the time to 10 minutes.
4. Do quick pressure release.

**Nutrition information:** Calories per serving: 166; Carbohydrates: 6.1g; Protein: 6.9g; Fat: 14.1g; Sugar: 0g; Sodium: 56mg; Fiber: 4.2g

# Slow-cooked Garlic Wings

Serves:    12

Preparation Time: 5 minutes

Cooking Time: 6 hours

## Ingredients

- 12 chicken wings
- 2 tablespoons avocado oil
- 1 tablespoon garlic powder
- 1 teaspoon salt
- 1 teaspoon pepper

## Instructions

1. Place all ingredients in the Instant Pot.
2. Give a good stir.
3. Close the lid and make sure that the vent points to "Venting."
4. Press the "Slow Cook" button and adjust the time to 6 hours.

**Nutrition information:** Calories per serving: 61; Carbohydrates: 0.9g; Protein: 6.6g; Fat:13.2g; Sugar:0 g; Sodium: 218mg; Fiber: 0g

# Seafood and Poultry Recipes

## Slow-cooked Sardines in Oil

Serves:   8

Preparation Time: 5 minutes

Cooking Time: 12 hours

### Ingredients

- 8 fresh sardines, gutted and heads removed
- ½ cup extra-virgin olive oil
- 1 bay leaf
- Salt and pepper to taste
- Juice of ½ lemon, freshly squeezed

### Instructions

1. Place all ingredients in the Instant Pot.
2. Pour in ½ cup of water.
3. Give a good stir.
4. Close the lid and make sure that the vent points to "Venting."
5. Press the "Slow Cook" button and adjust the time to 12 hours.

**Nutrition information:** Calories per serving: 80; Carbohydrates: 0.7g; Protein: 3.1g; Fat: 7.2g; Sugar: 0g; Sodium: 12mg; Fiber: 0.3g

# Crab-Stuffed Avocado

Serves: 5

Preparation Time: 10 minutes

Cooking Time: 5 minutes

## Ingredients

- 1-pound crab
- 1 ripe avocado, pitted and peeled
- 2 tablespoons onion, chopped finely
- 2 tablespoons cilantro, chopped
- Salt and pepper to taste

## Instructions

1. Place the crab in the Instant Pot and add a cup of water.
2. Close the lid and make sure that the vent points to "Sealing."
3. Press the "Manual" button and adjust the time to 5 minutes.
4. Do quick pressure release.
5. Take the crab out and let it cool.
6. Extract the meat from the crab and discard the shells.
7. In a bowl, combine the crabmeat and stir in the rest of the ingredients.
8. Refrigerate.
9. Serve chilled.

**Nutrition information:** Calories per serving: 149; Carbohydrates: 4.7g; Protein: 13.2g; Fat: 15.3g; Sugar: 0g; Sodium: 270mg; Fiber:2.8g

# Keto Spicy Prawns

Serves:   4

Preparation Time: 5 minutes

Cooking Time: 5 minutes

## Ingredients

- 3 tablespoons olive oil
- 1 tablespoon butter
- ½ pound prawns
- 1 tablespoon red pepper flakes
- 3 cloves of garlic, minced

## Instructions

1. Place all ingredients in the Instant Pot.
2. Add ¼ cup of water and season with salt and pepper to taste.
3. Close the lid and make sure that the vent points to "Sealing."
4. Press the "Manual" button and adjust the time to 5 minutes.
5. Do quick pressure release.

**Nutrition information:** Calories per serving: 174; Carbohydrates: 2.4g; Protein:8.9g; Fat: 15.2g; Sugar: 0g; Sodium: 496mg; Fiber: 1.3g

# Savory Steamed Salmon

Serves:   2

Preparation Time: 10 minutes

Cooking Time: 10 minutes

## Ingredients

- 1/3 cup olive oil
- 2 tablespoons butter
- 2 salmon fillets
- 1 tablespoon fresh lemon juice
- 2 tablespoons dill

## Instructions

1. Place a steam rack in the Instant Pot and pour in a cup of water.
2. Place all ingredients in a heat-proof dish and season with salt and pepper to taste.
3. Place the dish with the salmon on the steam rack.
4. Close the lid and make sure that the vent points to "Sealing."
5. Press the "Steam" button and adjust the time to 10 minutes.
6. Do quick pressure release.

**Nutrition information:** Calories per serving: 914; Carbohydrates: 4.1g; Protein: 63.2g; Fat: 80.9g; Sugar: 0g; Sodium: 291mg; Fiber: 2.5g

# Keto Tuna Salad

Serves:    4

Preparation Time: 10 minutes

Cooking Time: 10 minutes

## Ingredients

- ½ pound tuna, cut into chunks
- 1 tablespoon fresh lemon juice
- 2 eggs, whole
- 1 small head lettuce
- 4 tablespoon olive oil

## Instructions

1. Season the tuna with lemon juice, salt and pepper.
2. Place in a baking dish that will fit inside the Instant Pot.
3. Place the eggs in the Instant Pot and add a cup of water.
4. Add a steam rack and put the baking dish with the tuna on top.
5. Close the lid and make sure that the vent points to "Sealing."
6. Press the "Steam" button and adjust the time to 10 minutes.
7. Do quick pressure release.
8. Allow the eggs and tuna to cool.
9. Peel the eggs and slice into wedges. Set aside.
10. Assemble the salad by shredding the lettuce in a salad bowl.
11. Toss in the cooled tuna and eggs.
12. Drizzle with olive oil and season with more salt and pepper to taste.

**Nutrition information:** Calories per serving: 260; Carbohydrates: 6.3g; Protein: 17.2g; Fat: 19.9g; Sugar: 0.2g; Sodium: 210mg; Fiber: 4.4g

# Keto Fish Casserole

Serves:   6

Preparation Time: 5 minutes

Cooking Time: 6 hours

## Ingredients

- 2 tablespoons olive oil
- 1 cup broccoli florets
- 1½ pounds halibut fillets, sliced into strips
- 1 tablespoon Dijon mustard
- 1¼ cup full-fat coconut cream

## Instructions

1. Place all ingredients in the Instant Pot and season with salt and pepper to taste.
2. Give a good stir.
3. Close the lid and make sure that the vent points to "Venting."
4. Press the "Slow Cook" button and adjust the time to 6 hours.

**Nutrition information:** Calories per serving: 419; Carbohydrates: 3.7g; Protein: 18.4g; Fat: 37.7g; Sugar: 0g; Sodium: 124mg; Fiber: 1.9g

# Thai Fish Curry

Serves:   6

Preparation Time: 5 minutes

Cooking Time: 10 minutes

## Ingredients

- 1/3 cup olive oil
- 1½ pounds salmon fillets
- 2 cups coconut milk, freshly squeezed
- 2 tablespoons curry powder
- ¼ cup chopped cilantro

## Instructions

1. Place all ingredients in the Instant Pot and season with salt and pepper to taste.
2. Give a good stir.
3. Close the lid and make sure that the vent points to "Sealing."
4. Press the "Manual" button and adjust the time to 10 minutes.
5. Do quick pressure release.

**Nutrition information:** Calories per serving: 470; Carbohydrates: 5.6g; Protein: 25.5g; Fat: 39.8g; Sugar: 0.9g; Sodium: 505mg; Fiber: 3.5g

# Salmon with Basil Pesto

Serves:   6

Preparation Time: 5 minutes

Cooking Time: 6 hours

## Ingredients

- 2 cups basil leaves
- ½ cup olive oil
- 2 tablespoons lemon juice, freshly squeezed
- 3 cloves of garlic, minced
- 1½ pounds salmon fillets

## Instructions

1. In a food processor, place the basil leaves, olive oil, lemon juice, and garlic. Season with salt and pepper to taste. Adjust the moisture by adding a few tablespoons of water. Pulse until smooth.
2. Place the salmon fillets in the Instant Pot and add the pesto sauce.
3. Close the lid and make sure that the vent points to "Venting."
4. Press the "Slow Cook" button and adjust the time to 6 hours.

**Nutrition information:** Calories per serving: 336; Carbohydrates: 0.9g; Protein:20.5 g; Fat: 28.1g; Sugar: 0g; Sodium: 493mg; Fiber: 0.4g

# Salmon Tandoori

Serves:  4

Preparation Time: 2 hours

Cooking Time: 6 hours

## Ingredients

- 1½ pounds salmon fillets
- 1 tablespoon tandoori spice mix
- 3 tablespoons coconut oil
- Salt and pepper to taste

## Instructions

1. Place all ingredients in a bowl and allow the fish to marinate for at least 2 hours in the refrigerator.
2. Place the marinated salmon in the Instant Pot.
3. Close the lid and make sure that the vent points to "Venting."
4. Press the "Slow Cook" button and adjust the time to 6 hours.
5. Halfway through the cooking time, open the lid and turn over the fish.
6. Continue cooking until the fish is done.

**Nutrition information:** Calories per serving: 354; Carbohydrates:1.4 g; Protein: 22.4g; Fat: 35.2g; Sugar: 0g; Sodium: 754mg; Fiber: 0.7g

# Instant Pot Curried Salmon

Serves: 4

Preparation Time: 5 minutes

Cooking Time: 13 minutes

## Ingredients

- 2 tablespoons coconut oil
- 1½ tablespoon minced garlic
- 1 onion, chopped
- 1 pound raw salmon, diced
- 2 cups coconut milk, freshly squeezed

## Instructions

1. Press the "Sauté" button on the Instant Pot and heat the oil.
2. Sauté the garlic and onions until fragrant.
3. Add the salmon and stir for 1 minute.
4. Pour in the coconut milk.
5. Close the lid and make sure that the vent points to "Sealing."
6. Press the "Manual" button and adjust the time to 10 minutes.
7. Do quick pressure release.

**Nutrition information:** Calories per serving: 524; Carbohydrates: 10.3g; Protein: 26.7g; Fat: 43.6g; Sugar: 1.2g; Sodium: 511mg; Fiber: 5.9g

# Instant Pot Fish en Papillote

Serves:   1

Preparation Time: 5 minutes

Cooking Time: 10 minutes

## Ingredients

- 1 3-ounce halibut fillet
- 4 tablespoons butter
- Salt and pepper to taste
- A dash of paprika
- Lemon wedges

## Instructions

1. Place a steam rack in the Instant Pot and pour in a cup of water.
2. Place the halibut fillet in the middle of a big sheet of aluminum foil. Season with butter, salt, pepper, and paprika.
3. Arrange the lemon wedges on top of the fish.
4. Fold the aluminum sheet to cover the fish and crimp the edges.
5. Place on the steam rack.
6. Close the lid and make sure that the vent points to "Sealing."
7. Press the "Steam" button and adjust the time to 10 minutes.
8. Do natural pressure release.

**Nutrition information:** Calories per serving: 594; Carbohydrates: 7.6g; Protein: 13.7g; Fat: 58.1g; Sugar: 0.7g; Sodium: 468mg; Fiber: 4.2g

# Buttered Trout

Serves:  2

Preparation Time: 5 minutes

Cooking Time: 6 hours

## Ingredients

- 1 large trout fillet
- 1 tablespoon olive oil
- 3 tablespoons butter
- Salt and pepper to taste
- 1 tablespoon orange zest

## Instructions

1. Place all ingredients in the Instant Pot.
2. Close the lid and make sure that the vent points to "Venting."
3. Press the "Slow Cook" button and adjust the time to 6 hours.
4. Halfway through the cooking time, open the lid and turn over the fish.
5. Continue cooking until the trout forms a hard crust on the surface.

**Nutrition information:** Calories per serving: 284; Carbohydrates: 3.1g; Protein: 6.6g; Fat: 27.9g; Sugar: 0g; Sodium: 159mg;

# Salmon Meatballs Soup

Serves:　5

Preparation Time: 5 minutes

Cooking Time: 10 minutes

## Ingredients

- 1 pound ground salmon
- 2 tablespoons butter
- 2 cloves of garlic, minced
- 2 large eggs, beaten
- 2 cups hot water

## Instructions

1. In a mixing bowl, combine the first four ingredients and season with salt and pepper to taste.
2. Combine the mixture and use your hands to form small balls.
3. Place the fish balls in the freezer to set for 2 hours or until frozen.
4. Pour the hot water in the Instant Pot and drop in the frozen fish balls.
5. Season with salt and pepper to taste.
6. Close the lid and make sure that the vent points to "Sealing."
7. Press the "Manual" button and adjust the time to 10 minutes.

**Nutrition information:** Calories per serving: 199; Carbohydrates: 0.6g; Protein: 13.3g; Fat: 19.4g; Sugar: 0g; Sodium: 95mg; Fiber:0.4g

# Salmon with Lemon and Butter

Serves:  5

Preparation Time: 5 minutes

Cooking Time: 6 hours

## Ingredients

- 3 tablespoons olive oil
- 1½ pounds salmon fillets
- 1 tablespoon Italian herb seasoning mix
- 3 tablespoons lemon juice, freshly squeezed
- 2 tablespoons butter

## Instructions

1. Place all ingredients in the Instant Pot.
2. Season with salt and pepper to taste and add 1/3 cup of water.
3. Close the lid and make sure that the vent points to "Venting."
4. Press the "Slow Cook" button and adjust the time to 6 hours.
5. Halfway through the cooking time, open the lid and turn over the fish.

**Nutrition information:** Calories per serving: 328; Carbohydrates: 1.6g; Protein: 22.5g; Fat: 28.3g; Sugar: 0g; Sodium: 750mg; Fiber: 0.6g

# Spicy Chili Garlic Trout

Serves:   9

Preparation Time: 5 minutes

Cooking Time: 6 hours

## Ingredients

- 2½ pounds trout fillets
- 3 tablespoons olive oil
- 6 cloves garlic, minced
- 1 teaspoon crushed red pepper flakes
- Salt and pepper to taste

## Instructions

1. Place all ingredients in the Instant Pot and adjust the moisture by adding ¼ cup of water.
2. Close the lid and make sure that the vent points to "Venting."
3. Press the "Slow Cook" button and adjust the time to 6 hours.

**Nutrition information:** Calories per serving: 182; Carbohydrates: 0.9g; Protein:12.4g; Fat: 15.6g; Sugar: 0g; Sodium: 417mg; Fiber: 0.5g

# Easy Baked Salmon in The Instant Pot

Serves:   4

Preparation Time: 5 minutes

Cooking Time: 6 hours

## Ingredients

- 4 6-ounce salmon fillet pieces
- 1½ teaspoon olive oil
- Salt and pepper to taste
- 2 tablespoons lemon juice, freshly squeezed

## Instructions

1. Place a sheet of aluminum foil in the Instant Pot.
2. Season the salmon fillets with olive oil, salt, pepper, and lemon juice.
3. Place gently on top of the foil.
4. Close the lid and make sure that the vent points to "Venting."
5. Press the "Slow Cook" button and adjust the time to 6 hours.
6. Halfway through the cooking time, turn over the fish and continue cooking until done.

**Nutrition information:** Calories per serving: 281; Carbohydrates: 1.6g; Protein: 25.4g; Fat: 27.9g; Sugar: 0g; Sodium: 737mg; Fiber: 1.2g

# Slow Cooker Italian Buttered Salmon

Serves: 5

Preparation Time: 5 minutes

Cooking Time: 6 hours

## Ingredients

- 1¼ pounds salmon
- 2 tablespoons lemon juice
- 4 tablespoons butter
- ¼ teaspoon Italian seasoning mix
- 1 tablespoon chopped parsley

## Instructions

1. Mix all ingredients in the Instant Pot and adjust the moisture by adding a few tablespoons of water.
2. Close the lid and make sure that the vent points to "Venting."
3. Press the "Slow Cook" button and adjust the time to 6 hours.
4. Halfway through the cooking time, turn over the fish and continue cooking until done.

**Nutrition information:** Calories per serving: 257; Carbohydrates: 0.6g; Protein: 17.3g; Fat: 23.5g; Sugar: 0g; Sodium: 575mg; Fiber: 0.2g

# Creamy Turmeric Shrimps

Serves:    3

Preparation Time: 5 minutes

Cooking Time: 4 hours

## Ingredients

- 1 cup coconut milk, freshly squeezed
- 1 thumb-sized ginger, sliced
- ½ pound prawns, peeled and deveined
- 1 tablespoon turmeric
- 4 cloves of garlic, minced

## Instructions

1. Mix all ingredients in the Instant Pot and adjust the moisture by adding a few tablespoons of water.
2. Close the lid and make sure that the vent points to "Venting."
3. Press the "Slow Cook" button and adjust the time to 4 hours.

**Nutrition information:** Calories per serving: 212; Carbohydrates: 4.3; Protein: 12.9g; Fat: 20.2g; Sugar:0.9g; Sodium: 671mg; Fiber: 2.3g

# Garlic Buttered Squid Rings

Serves:  5

Preparation Time: 5 minutes

Cooking Time: 4 hours

## Ingredients

- 1pound squid, cleaned and cut into rings
- 1 stick butter
- 6 cloves of garlic, minced
- 1 teaspoon crushed red pepper flakes
- Salt and pepper to taste

## Instructions

1. Mix all ingredients in the Instant Pot and adjust the moisture by adding a few tablespoons of water.
2. Close the lid and make sure that the vent points to "Venting."
3. Press the "Slow Cook" button and adjust the time to 4 hours.

**Nutrition information:** Calories per serving: 324; Carbohydrates: 5.6g; Protein: 16.2g; Fat: 30.1g; Sugar: 0.8g; Sodium: 243mg; Fiber: 3.2g

# Garlicky Greek Chicken

Serves:  4

Preparation Time: 5 minutes

Cooking Time: 20 minutes

## Ingredients

- 3 tablespoons extra-virgin olive oil
- 3 cloves of garlic, minced
- 1 pound chicken thighs
- 1 teaspoon dried oregano
- 1 lemon, sliced

## Instructions

1. Place all ingredients in the Instant Pot.
2. Add ½ cup of water and season with salt and pepper to taste.
3. Close the lid and make sure that the vent points to "Sealing."
4. Press the "Poultry" button and adjust the time to 20 minutes.
5. Do natural pressure release.

**Nutrition information:** Calories per serving: 298; Carbohydrates: 2.1g; Protein: 16.5g; Fat: 23.3g; Sugar: 0g; Sodium: 182mg; Fiber: 1.3g

# Pork and Beef Recipes

## Adobo Pork Chops

Serves:   5

Preparation Time: 5 minutes

Cooking Time: 50 minutes

### Ingredients

- 1 pound pork chops
- ½ cup coconut aminos
- ¼ cup lemon juice, freshly squeezed
- 3 cloves garlic, minced
- 3 tablespoons olive oil

### Instructions

1. Place all ingredients in the Instant Pot.
2. Season with salt and pepper if necessary and add ¼ cup of water.
3. Close the lid and make sure that the vent points to "Sealing."
4. Press the "Meat/Stew" button and adjust the time to 50 minutes.
5. Do natural pressure release.

**Nutrition information:** Calories per serving:271; Carbohydrates: 2.3g; Protein: 18.2g; Fat: 23.3g; Sugar: 0g; Sodium: 76mg; Fiber: 1.5g

# Mexican Pulled Pork

Serves:   15

Preparation Time: 5 minutes

Cooking Time: 90 minutes

## Ingredients

- 4 pounds pork shoulder
- 1 teaspoon cinnamon
- 2 teaspoons garlic powder
- 1 teaspoon cumin powder
- 5 tablespoons coconut oil

## Instructions

1. Place all ingredients in the Instant Pot and pour 1 ½ cups of water.
2. Season with salt and pepper to taste.
3. Close the lid and make sure that the vent points to "Sealing."
4. Press the "Meat/Stew" button and adjust the time to 1 hour and 30 minutes.
5. Do natural pressure release.
6. Once the lid is open, take the meat out and shred using two forks.

**Nutrition information:** Calories per serving: 364; Carbohydrates: 0.5g; Protein: 20.4g; Fat: 35.9g; Sugar: 0g; Sodium: 71mg; Fiber: 0g

# Italian Pork Cutlets

Serves:   6

Preparation Time: 5 minutes

Cooking Time: 55 minutes

## Ingredients

- 6 pork cutlets
- 1 tablespoon Italian herb mix (rosemary, oregano, and thyme)
- Salt and pepper to taste
- 4 tablespoons olive oil
- 1 cup water

## Instructions

1. Place all ingredients in the Instant Pot and add 1½ cups of water.
2. Close the lid and make sure that the vent points to "Sealing."
3. Press the "Meat/Stew" button and adjust the time to 55 minutes.
4. Do natural pressure release.

**Nutrition information:** Calories per serving: 322; Carbohydrates: 0.9g; Protein: 19.4g; Fat: 34.6g; Sugar: 0g; Sodium: 699mg; Fiber: 0.4g

# Pork with Paprika and Mushrooms

Serves:    6

Preparation Time: 5 minutes

Cooking Time: 8 hours

## Ingredients

- 4 tablespoons olive oil
- 1 pound pork loin
- 1 tablespoon thyme
- 2 tablespoons paprika
- 1 cup sliced cremini mushrooms

## Instructions

1. Press the "Sauté" button on the Instant Pot and heat the oil.
2. Sear the pork loin on all sides for 3 minutes.
3. Add the thyme, paprika, and mushrooms.
4. Season with salt and pepper to taste and add ½ cup of water.
5. Close the lid and make sure that the vent points to "Venting."
6. Press the "Slow Cook" button and adjust the time to 8 hours.

**Nutrition information:** Calories per serving: 245; Carbohydrates: 1.3g; Protein: 17.3g; Fat: 19.8g; Sugar: 0g; Sodium: 43mg; Fiber:0.6g

# Ketogenic Pork Vindaloo

Serves:    9

Preparation Time: 5 minutes

Cooking Time: 60 minutes

## Ingredients

- ¼ cup coconut oil
- 2 pounds pork shoulder, cut into chunks
- 1 tablespoon garam masala
- 1 cup water
- 3 tablespoons lemon juice, freshly squeezed

## Instructions

1. Press the "Sauté" button on the Instant Pot and heat the oil.
2. Sear the pork loin on all sides for 3 minutes.
3. Add the garam masala and continue stirring for 2 more minutes.
4. Stir in the rest of the ingredients.
5. Close the lid and make sure that the vent points to "Sealing."
6. Press the "Meat/Stew" button and adjust the time to 55 minutes.
7. Do natural pressure release.

**Nutrition information:** Calories per serving: 322; Carbohydrates: 0.4g; Protein: 23.9g; Fat: 25.2g; Sugar: 0g; Sodium: 59mg; Fiber: 0g

# Pork Coconut Curry

Serves:   9

Preparation Time: 5 minutes

Cooking Time: 50 minutes

## Ingredients

- 3 tablespoons coconut oil
- 3 cloves of garlic, minced
- 1 tablespoon garam masala
- 2 pounds pork shoulders, cut into chunks
- 1 cup coconut milk, freshly squeezed

## Instructions

1. Press the "Sauté" button on the Instant Pot and heat the oil.
2. Sauté the garlic and garam masala until fragrant.
3. Add the meat and allow to sear on all sides for 3 minutes.
4. Pour in the coconut milk.
5. Close the lid and make sure that the vent points to "Sealing."
6. Press the "Meat/Stew" button and adjust the time to 45 minutes.
7. Do natural pressure release.

**Nutrition information:** Calories per serving: 371; Carbohydrates: 1.8g; Protein: 23.4g; Fat: 28.7g; Sugar: 0g; Sodium: 64mg; Fiber: 0.5g

# Spicy Pulled Pork

Serves:   6

Preparation Time: 5 minutes

Cooking Time: 12 hours and 5 minutes

## Ingredients

- 1 pound pork shoulder, bone removed
- 1 tablespoon cayenne pepper
- 1 teaspoon garlic
- 1 teaspoon paprika
- 1 cup coconut milk

## Instructions

1. Place the pork shoulder, cayenne pepper, garlic, and paprika in the Instant Pot.
2. Season with salt and pepper to taste and pour in a cup of water.
3. Close the lid and make sure that the vent points to "Venting."
4. Press the "Slow Cook" button and adjust the time to 12 hours.
5. Once cooked, take the meat out and shred using two forks.
6. Return the meat to the Instant Pot and pour in the coconut milk.
7. Close the lid and make sure that the vent points to "Sealing."
8. Press the "Meat/Stew" button and adjust the time to 5 minutes.
9. Do natural pressure release.

**Nutrition information:** Calories per serving:298; Carbohydrates: 3.1g; Protein: 20.1g; Fat: 23.6g; Sugar: 0g; Sodium: 52mg; Fiber: 2.1g

# Keto Mustard Pork Casserole

Serves:  10

Preparation Time: 5 minutes

Cooking Time: 50 minutes

## Ingredients

- 4 tablespoons butter
- 2 pounds pork shoulder, cut into chunks
- 3 tablespoons yellow mustard
- 1 cup water
- 1 cup sliced mushrooms

## Instructions

1. Press the "Sauté" button on the Instant Pot and heat the butter.
2. Add the pork shoulder and mustard. Cook, stirring, for 3 minutes.
3. Stir in water and mushrooms.
4. Season with salt and pepper to taste.
5. Close the lid and make sure that the vent points to "Sealing."
6. Press the "Meat/Stew" button and adjust the time to 50 minutes.
7. Do natural pressure release.

**Nutrition information:** Calories per serving: 286; Carbohydrates: 0.3g; Protein: 22.9g; Fat: 20.8g; Sugar: 0g; Sodium: 141mg; Fiber: 0g

# Mexican Chili Pork

Serves:   9

Preparation Time: 5 minutes

Cooking Time: 50 minutes

## Ingredients

- 3 tablespoons olive oil
- 2 teaspoon minced garlic
- 2 pounds pork sirloin, cut into thick slices
- 2 teaspoons ground cumin
- 1 tablespoon red chili flakes

## Instructions

1. Press the "Sauté" button and heat the olive oil.
2. Sauté the garlic until fragrant.
3. Add the pork sirloin and stir for 3 minutes.
4. Add the cumin and chili flakes.
5. Pour in a cup of water and season with salt and pepper to taste.
6. Close the lid and make sure that the vent points to "Sealing."
7. Press the "Meat/Stew" button and adjust the time to 50 minutes.
8. Do natural pressure release.

**Nutrition information:** Calories per serving: 159; Carbohydrates: 0.8g; Protein: 21.1g; Fat: 16.8g; Sugar: 0g; Sodium: 77mg; Fiber: 0g

# Smokey And Spicy Instant Pot Roast

Serves:    12

Preparation Time: 5 minutes

Cooking Time: 1 hour and 30 minutes

## Ingredients

- 5 tablespoons olive oil
- 4 pounds pork butt
- 2 tablespoon liquid smoke
- 1 tablespoon cayenne pepper flakes
- Salt and pepper to taste

## Instructions

1. Place all ingredients in the Instant Pot.
2. Pour in a cup of water.
3. Close the lid and make sure that the vent points to "Sealing."
4. Press the "Meat/Stew" button and adjust the time to 1 hour and 30 minutes.
5. Do natural pressure release.

**Nutrition information:** Calories per serving: 456; Carbohydrates: 0.7g; Protein: 32.9g; Fat: 39g; Sugar: 0g; Sodium: 88mg; Fiber: 0.4g

# Pulled Pork Casserole

Serves:   4

Preparation Time: 5 minutes

Cooking Time: 8 hours

## Ingredients

- 4 cups leftover pulled pork (any recipe)
- ¼ cups olive oil
- 4 eggs, beaten
- ¼ teaspoon balsamic vinegar
- Salt and pepper to taste

## Instructions

1. In a mixing bowl, combine all ingredients until well incorporated.
2. Pour into the Instant Pot.
3. Close the lid and make sure that the vent points to "Venting."
4. Press the "Slow Cook" button and adjust the time to 8 hours.

**Nutrition information:** Calories per serving: 372; Carbohydrates: 2.1g; Protein: 21.7g; Fat: 32.2g; Sugar: 0g; Sodium: 132mg; Fiber: 1.3g

# Asian Lemongrass Pork

Serves:   10

Preparation Time: 5 minutes

Cooking Time: 1 hour

## Ingredients

- 4 tablespoons coconut oil
- 6 cloves of garlic
- 2 tablespoons lemongrass
- 2 pounds pork shoulder, cut into chunks
- ¼ cup fish sauce

## Instructions

1. Press the "Sauté" button and heat the coconut oil.
2. Sauté the garlic and lemongrass until fragrant.
3. Cook the pork chunks for 3 minutes, stirring, until all sides are seared.
4. Season with fish sauce and pour in a cup of water.
5. Close the lid and make sure that the vent points to "Sealing."
6. Press the "Meat/Stew" button and adjust the time to 55 minutes.
7. Do natural pressure release.

**Nutrition information:** Calories per serving: 249; Carbohydrates: 0.8g; Protein: 21.5g; Fat: 23.3g; Sugar: 0g; Sodium: 618mg; Fiber: 0.4g

# Pork Chops with Onions

Serves:   4

Preparation Time: 5 minutes

Cooking Time: 1 hour

## Ingredients

- 4 pork chops, bones removed
- 3 tablespoons butter
- 3 onions, chopped
- ½ cup broth
- ¼ cup heavy cream

## Instructions

1. Press the "Sauté" button on the Instant Pot.
2. Heat the butter and add the pork chops and onion.
3. Cook, stirring, until the pork is seared.
4. Stir in the broth and season with salt and pepper to taste.
5. Close the lid and make sure that the vent points to "Sealing."
6. Press the "Meat/Stew" button and adjust the time to 55 minutes.
7. Do quick pressure release.
8. Once the lid is open, add the heavy cream.
9. Press the "Sauté" button and allow to simmer for 5 minutes.

**Nutrition information:** Calories per serving: 468; Carbohydrates: 8.4g; Protein: 28.1g; Fat: 35.2g; Sugar: 0g; Sodium: 258mg; Fiber: 3.9g

# Indian Instant Pot Roasted Pork

Serves:     6

Preparation Time: 5 minutes

Cooking Time: 8 hours

## Ingredients

- 1 pound pork loin
- 1 onion, sliced
- 2 cloves of garlic, chopped roughly
- 1 teaspoon cumin
- ½ cup olive oil

## Instructions

1. Place the pork loin in the Instant Pot. Set aside.
2. In a food processor, place the remaining ingredients and season with salt and pepper to taste.
3. Pulse until smooth.
4. Pour over the pork loin.
5. Close the lid and make sure that the vent points to "Venting."
6. Press the "Slow Cook" button and adjust the time to 8 hours.

**Nutrition information:** Calories per serving: 321; Carbohydrates: 0.6g; Protein: 19.5g; Fat: 26.5g; Sugar: 0g; Sodium: 43mg; Fiber: 0.3g

# Instant Pot Ribs

Serves:  3

Preparation Time: 5 minutes

Cooking Time: 8 hours

## Ingredients

- 1 rack baby back ribs
- 1 tablespoon garlic powder
- 1 tablespoon onion powder
- 1 tablespoon smoked paprika
- 5 tablespoons olive oil

## Instructions

1. Place the baby back ribs on a baking sheet and season with the rest of the ingredients. Sprinkle with salt and pepper to taste.
2. Rub the ribs entirely with the spice mixture.
3. Place all ingredients in the Instant Pot.
4. Pour in ½ cup of water.
5. Close the lid and make sure that the vent points to "Venting."
6. Press the "Slow Cook" button and adjust the time to 8 hours.

**Nutrition information:** Calories per serving:1375; Carbohydrates: 6.4g; Protein: 98.2g; Fat: 104.7g; Sugar: 0g; Sodium: 313mg; Fiber: 4.8g

# Garlic Pork Tenderloin

Serves:   10

Preparation Time: 5 minutes

Cooking Time: 8 hours

## Ingredients

- 3 tablespoons extra-virgin olive oil
- ¼ cup butter
- 1 head garlic cloves, minced
- 1 teaspoon thyme
- 3 pounds pork tenderloin

## Instructions

1. Heat the oil and butter in the Instant Pot.
2. Sauté the garlic and thyme until fragrant.
3. Add the pork tenderloin and cook for 3 minutes, stirring.
4. Pour in a cup of water and season with salt and pepper to taste.
5. Close the lid and make sure that the vent points to "Venting."
6. Press the "Slow Cook" button and adjust the time to 8 hours.

**Nutrition information:** Calories per serving: 252; Carbohydrates: 0.2g; Protein: 11.8g; Fat: 35.6g; Sugar: 0g; Sodium: 155mg; Fiber: 0g

# Easy Chinese Pork

Serves:  4

Preparation Time: 5 minutes

Cooking Time: 55 minutes

## Ingredients

- 4 tablespoons coconut oil
- 4 cloves of garlic, minced
- 1 tablespoon ginger, fresh
- 4 boneless pork chops
- 2 tablespoons coconut aminos

## Instructions

1. Press the "Sauté" button on the Instant Pot and heat the oil.
2. Stir in the garlic and ginger until fragrant.
3. Add the pork and stir for 2 minutes.
4. Pour in the coconut aminos and season with salt and pepper to taste. Adjust the moisture by pouring in 1 cup of water.
5. Close the lid and make sure that the vent points to "Sealing."
6. Press the "Meat/Stew" button and adjust the time to 50 minutes.
7. Do quick pressure release.
8. Once the lid is open, press the "Sauté" button and allow to simmer until the sauce has thickened.

**Nutrition information:** Calories per serving: 359; Carbohydrates: 1.5g; Protein: 19.7g; Fat: 41.6g; Sugar: 0g; Sodium: 99mg; Fiber: 0.5g

# Basic Keto Pork Chops

Serves:    6

Preparation Time: 5 minutes

Cooking Time: 30 minutes

## Ingredients

- 8 tablespoons butter
- 3 cloves of garlic, minced
- 6 boneless pork chops
- ½ cup heavy cream
- ½ cup chicken broth

## Instructions

1. Press the "Sauté" button on the Instant Pot.
2. Heat the butter and sauté the garlic.
3. Add the pork chops and sear for 3 minutes on each side.
4. Add the heavy cream and broth.
5. Season with salt and pepper to taste.
6. Close the lid and make sure that the vent points to "Sealing."
7. Press the "Meat/Stew" button and adjust the time to 30 minutes.
8. Do quick pressure release.

**Nutrition information:** Calories per serving: 439; Carbohydrates: 0.9g; Protein: 26.7g; Fat: 46.2g; Sugar: 0g; Sodium: 299mg; Fiber: 0.3g

# Garlic and Parsley Pork Loin Roast

Serves:    12

Preparation Time: 5 minutes

Cooking Time: 1 hour or 30 minutes

## Ingredients

- 4 tablespoons olive oil
- 4 cloves of garlic
- ½ cup chopped paprika
- 3 pounds pork loin roast
- Salt and pepper to taste

## Instructions

1. Press the "Sauté" button on the Instant Pot.
2. Sauté the garlic and paprika until fragrant.
3. Add the pork loin roast and sear on all sides for 3 minutes.
4. Season with salt and pepper to taste.
5. Pour in a cup of water.
6. Close the lid and make sure that the vent points to "Sealing."
7. Press the "Meat/Stew" button and adjust the time to 1 hour and 30 minutes.
8. Do quick pressure release.

**Nutrition information:** Calories per serving: 273; Carbohydrates: 3.1g; Protein:20.7g; Fat: 22.8g; Sugar: 0g; Sodium: 56mg; Fiber: 2.5g

# Asian Striped Pork

Serves:   4

Preparation Time: 5 minutes

Cooking Time: 30 minutes

## Ingredients

- 4 tablespoons avocado oil
- 2 cloves of garlic
- ½ pound pork sirloin, sliced into strips
- 1 tablespoon coconut aminos
- 2 tablespoons sesame oil

## Instructions

1. Press the "Sauté" button on the Instant pot and heat the avocado oil.
2. Sauté the garlic and stir in the pork sirloin.
3. Pour in the coconut aminos and season with salt and pepper to taste.
4. Adjust the moisture by adding ½ cup of water.
5. Close the lid and make sure that the vent points to "Sealing."
6. Press the "Meat/Stew" button and adjust the time to 30 minutes.
7. Do quick pressure release.
8. Once the lid is open, drizzle with sesame oil.

**Nutrition information:** Calories per serving: 251; Carbohydrates: 0.6g; Protein: 12.1g; Fat: 23.8g; Sugar: 0g; Sodium: 33mg; Fiber: 0.2g

# Desserts and Sweet Treats

## Cinnamon Butter Bites

Serves:   12

Preparation Time: 5 minutes

Cooking Time: 5 hours

### Ingredients

- 1 stick unsalted butter, grass-fed
- ¼ cup liquid stevia
- 1 tablespoon cinnamon
- 1 cup almond flour
- 5 eggs, beaten

### Instructions

1. Mix all ingredients in a mixing bowl.
2. Season with a pinch of salt.
3. Grease the inner pot.
4. Pour in the batter.
5. Close the lid and make sure that the vent points to "Venting."
6. Press the "Slow Cook" button and adjust the time to 5 hours.

**Nutrition information:** Calories per serving: 161; Carbohydrates: 1.2g; Protein: 4.5g; Fat: 15.5g; Sugar: 0g; Sodium: 50mg; Fiber: 0.7g

# Keto Almond Bread

Serves:   10

Preparation Time: 10 minutes

Cooking Time: 5 hours

## Ingredients

- 3 large eggs, beaten
- ¼ cup olive oil
- 2½ cups almond flour
- 1½ cups erythritol
- 1½ teaspoons baking powder

## Instructions

1. Mix all ingredients in a mixing bowl.
2. Add a pinch of salt and cinnamon if desired.
3. Once properly mixed, pour the batter in the greased Instant Pot.
4. Close the lid and make sure that the vent points to "Venting."
5. Press the "Slow Cook" button and adjust the time to 5 hours.

**Nutrition information:** Calories per serving: 67; Carbohydrates: 0.6g; Protein: 0.9g; Fat: 6.9g; Sugar: 0g; Sodium: 3mg; Fiber: 0.2g

# Chocolate Chia Pudding

Serves:    4

Preparation Time: 5 minutes

Cooking Time: 3 hours

## Ingredients

- 1 cup coconut milk, freshly squeezed
- ¼ cup chia seeds
- 2 tablespoons cacao powder
- ½ teaspoon liquid stevia
- A pinch of salt

## Instructions

1. Pour everything in the Instant Pot.
2. Give a good stir.
3. Close the lid and make sure that the vent points to "Venting."
4. Press the "Slow Cook" button and adjust the time to 3 hours.

**Nutrition information:** Calories per serving: 346; Carbohydrates: 21.2g; Protein: 8.4g; Fat: 27.5g; Sugar: 0.9g; Sodium: 16mg; Fiber: 17.3g

# Bulletproof Hot Choco

Serves:    1

Preparation Time: 5 minutes

Cooking Time: 5 minutes

## Ingredients

- ½ cup coconut milk
- 2 tablespoons coconut oil
- 2 tablespoons cocoa powder, unsweetened
- A dash of cinnamon
- 1 teaspoon erythritol

## Instructions

1. Place the coconut oil in the Instant Pot.
2. Pour ½ cup of water.
3. Close the lid and make sure that the vent points to "Sealing."
4. Press the "Manual" button and adjust the time to 5 minutes.
5. Do quick pressure release.
6. Open the lid and press the "Sauté" button.
7. Stir in the coconut oil, cocoa powder, cinnamon and erythritol.

**Nutrition information:** Calories per serving: 534; Carbohydrates:12.9 g; Protein: 4.7g; Fat: 57.2g; Sugar: 1.8g; Sodium: 20mg; Fiber: 8.3g

# Coconut Boosters

Serves:     5

Preparation Time: 2 hours

Cooking Time: 5 minutes

## Ingredients

- 1 cup coconut oil
- ½ cup chia seeds
- 1 teaspoon vanilla extract
- 1 teaspoon erythritol
- ¼ cup dried coconut flakes, unsweetened

## Instructions

1. Press the "Sauté" button on the Instant Pot.
2. Heat the coconut oil and add the chia seeds, vanilla extract, erythritol, and coconut flakes.
3. Stir for 5 minutes.
4. Scoop into balls and place on a baking sheet.
5. Allow to set in the refrigerator for 2 hours before serving.

**Nutrition information:** Calories per serving: 480; Carbohydrates: 9.4g; Protein: 2.9g; Fat: 50g; Sugar: 1.2g; Sodium: 15mg; Fiber: 5.9g

# Keto Brownies

Serves:    9

Preparation Time: 10 minutes

Cooking Time: 5 hours

## Ingredients

- ½ cup coconut oil
- 5 eggs, beaten
- 1/3 cup dark chocolate chips
- ¼ cup almond flour
- 2 teaspoons erythritol

## Instructions

1. Place all ingredients in a mixing bowl.
2. Season with a pinch of salt.
3. Make sure the contents are well combined.
4. Pour into the greased Instant Pot.
5. Close the lid and make sure that the vent points to "Venting."
6. Press the "Slow Cook" button and adjust the time to 5 hours.

**Nutrition information:** Calories per serving: 214; Carbohydrates: 3.4g; Protein: 5.4g; Fat: 20.7g; Sugar: 0g; Sodium: 58mg; Fiber: 1.9g

# Chocolate Mug Cake

Serves:   1

Preparation Time: 10 minutes

Cooking Time: 10 minutes

## Ingredients

- 1 egg, beaten
- ¼ cup almond powder
- ¼ teaspoon baking powder
- 1½ tablespoon cocoa powder
- Liquid stevia to taste

## Instructions

1. Place a steam rack in the Instant Pot and pour in a cup of water.
2. Place all ingredients in a mixing bowl. Add a pinch of salt.
3. Mix until well combined.
4. Pour into a heat-proof mug.
5. Place the mug on the steam rack.
6. Close the lid and make sure that the vent points to "Sealing."
7. Press the "Steam" button and adjust the time to 10 minutes.

**Nutrition information:** Calories per serving: 149; Carbohydrates: 5.8g; Protein: 6.8g; Fat: 10.5g; Sugar: 1.2g; Sodium: 104mg; Fiber: 2.3g

# Ketogenic Vanilla Jell-O

Serves:   6

Preparation Time: 2 hours

Cooking Time: 6 minutes

## Ingredients

- 1 cup boiling water
- 2 tablespoons gelatin powder, unsweetened
- 3 tablespoons erythritol
- 1 cup heavy cream
- 1 teaspoon vanilla extract

## Instructions

1. Place the boiling water in the Instant Pot.
2. Press the "Sauté" button on the Instant Pot and allow the water to simmer.
3. Add the gelatin powder and allow to dissolve.
4. Stir in the rest of the ingredients.
5. Pour the mixture into Jell-O molds.
6. Place in the refrigerator to set for 2 hours.

**Nutrition information:** Calories per serving: 105; Carbohydrates: 5.2g; Protein: 3.3; Fat: 7.9g; Sugar: 0g; Sodium: 31mg; Fiber:3.4g

# Nut-Free Keto Fudge

Serves:    15

Preparation Time: 5 minutes

Cooking Time: 4hours

## Ingredients

- 6 eggs, beaten
- 1 stick of butter, melted
- ¼ cup cocoa powder
- ½ teaspoon baking powder
- 4 tablespoons erythritol

## Instructions

1. Mix all ingredients in a bowl.
2. Add a pinch of salt.
3. Mix until well combined.
4. Pour into greased Instant Pot.
5. Close the lid and make sure that the vent points to "Venting."
6. Press the "Slow Cook" button and adjust the time to 4 hours.

**Nutrition information:** Calories per serving:131; Carbohydrates:1.3 g; Protein: 4.3g; Fat: 12.2g; Sugar: 0g; Sodium: 109mg; Fiber: 0.9g

# Coconut Pudding

Serves:   2

Preparation Time: 5 minutes

Cooking Time: 3 hours

## Ingredients

- ½ cup coconut milk
- ¼ cup dried coconut flakes
- ½ teaspoon cinnamon powder
- A dash of vanilla extract
- 1 teaspoon erythritol

## Instructions

1. Place all ingredients in the Instant Pot.
2. Add a pinch of salt and ½ cup water.
3. Mix until well combined.
4. Close the lid and make sure that the vent points to "Venting."
5. Press the "Slow Cook" button and adjust the time to 3 hours.

**Nutrition information:** Calories per serving: 188; Carbohydrates: 9.3g; Protein: 1.7g; Fat: 17.3g; Sugar: 0g; Sodium: 39mg; Fiber: 6.3g

# Sauces and Dressings

## Ketogenic Cheese Sause

Serves:   4

Preparation Time: 5 minutes

Cooking Time: 4 hours

### Ingredients

- ¼ cup heavy cream
- 2 tablespoons butter
- ¼ cup cream cheese
- ½ cup grated cheddar cheese
- Salt and pepper to taste

### Instructions

1. Place all ingredients in the Instant Pot.
2. Mix to combine all ingredients.
3. Close the lid and make sure that the vent points to "Venting."
4. Press the "Slow Cook" button and adjust the time to 4 hours.

**Nutrition information:** Calories per serving: 250; Carbohydrates:5.3 g; Protein: 10.9g; Fat: 20.3g; Sugar: 2.6g; Sodium: 894mg; Fiber: 0.9g

# Chimichurri Sauce

Serves:    6

Preparation Time: 5 minutes

Cooking Time: 3 hours

## Ingredients

- 1 lemon, zest and juice
- ½ yellow bell pepper, chopped
- 1 green chili pepper, chopped
- 1 cup olive oil
- 2 garlic cloves, minced

## Instructions

1. Place all ingredients in the Instant Pot.
2. Close the lid and make sure that the vent points to "Venting."
3. Press the "Slow Cook" button and adjust the time to 3 hours.

**Nutrition information:** Calories per serving: 326; Carbohydrates: 1.9g; Protein: 0.3g; Fat: 36.5g; Sugar: 0g; Sodium: 2mg; Fiber: 0.9g

# Chili Aioli

Serves: 6

Preparation Time: 5 minutes

Cooking Time: 2 minutes

## Ingredients

- 1 egg yolk
- 2 cloves of garlic, minced
- ¾ cup avocado oil
- ½ teaspoon chili flakes
- 1 tablespoon lemon juice

## Instructions

1. Place all ingredients in the Instant Pot and whisk vigorously.
2. Press the "Sauté" button and allow to heat up for 2 minutes while stirring.
3. Do not allow to boil.
4. Pour into container and store in the refrigerator for up to 2 weeks.

**Nutrition information:** Calories per serving:253; Carbohydrates: 0.7g; Protein: 0.5g; Fat: 28.1g; Sugar: 0g; Sodium: 8mg; Fiber: 0g

# Keto Ranch Dip

Serves:    8

Preparation Time: 5 minutes

Cooking Time: 2 minutes

## Ingredients

- 1 cup egg whites, beaten
- 1 lemon, juice, freshly squeezed
- Salt and pepper to taste
- 1 teaspoon mustard paste
- 1 cup olive oil

## Instructions

1. Place all ingredients in the Instant Pot and whisk vigorously.
2. Press the "Sauté" button and allow to heat up for 2 minutes while stirring.
3. Do not allow to simmer.
4. Pour into a container and store in the refrigerator for 2 weeks.

**Nutrition information:** Calories per serving: 258; Carbohydrates: 1.2g; Protein: 3.4g; Fat: 27.1g; Sugar: 0g; Sodium: 58mg; Fiber: 0.7g

# Keto Hollandaise Sauce

Serves:    4

Preparation Time: 5 minutes

Cooking Time: 5 minutes

## Ingredients

- 2/3 pounds butter
- 4 egg yolks, beaten
- 2 tablespoons lemon juice
- Salt and pepper to taste

## Instructions

1. Press the Sauté button on the Instant Pot.
2. Add the butter and allow to melt.
3. Whisk vigorously while adding the yolks.
4. Turn off the Instant Pot after 1 minute.
5. Continue stirring and add the lemon juice and seasoning.

**Nutrition information:** Calories per serving: 606; Carbohydrates: 2.2g; Protein: 3.5g; Fat: 66.8g; Sugar: 0g; Sodium: 498mg; Fiber: 1.5g

# Ketogenic-Friendly Gravy

Serves:  6

Preparation Time: 5 minutes

Cooking Time: 10 minutes

## Ingredients

- 2 tablespoons butter
- 1 white onion, chopped
- ¼ cup coconut milk
- 2 cups bone broth
- 1 tablespoon balsamic vinegar

## Instructions

1. Press the "Sauté" button on the Instant Pot.
2. Melt the butter and sauté the onions for 2 minutes.
3. Add the rest of the ingredients.
4. Stir constantly for 5 minutes or until slightly thickened.

**Nutrition information:** Calories per serving: 59; Carbohydrates: 1.1g; Protein: 0.2g; Fat: 6.3g; Sugar: 0g; Sodium: 33mg; Fiber:0 g

# Ketogenic Satay Sauce

Serves:   6

Preparation Time: 5 minutes

Cooking Time: 3 hours

## Ingredients

- 1 cup coconut milk
- 1 red chili pepper, chopped finely
- 1 clove of garlic, minced
- 4 tablespoons coconut aminos
- 1/3 cup peanut butter

## Instructions

1. Place all ingredients in the Instant Pot.
2. Stir to combine everything.
3. Close the lid and make sure that the vent points to "Venting."
4. Press the "Slow Cook" button and adjust the time to 3 hours.

**Nutrition information:** Calories per serving: 138; Carbohydrates: 6.9g; Protein: 2.1g; Fat: 12.3g; Sugar: 1.2g; Sodium: 229mg; Fiber: 3.4g

# Béarnaise Sauce

Serves:    4

Preparation Time: 5 minutes

Cooking Time: 3 minutes

## Ingredients

- 2/3 pounds butter
- 4 egg yolks, beaten
- 2 teaspoons lemon juice, freshly squeezed
- ¼ teaspoon onion powder
- 2 tablespoon fresh tarragon

## Instructions

1. Press the "Sauté" button on the Instant Pot.
2. Melt the butter for 3 minutes.
3. Transfer into a mixing bowl.
4. While whisking the melted butter, slowly add the egg yolks.
5. Continue stirring so that no lumps form.
6. Add the lemon juice, onion powder, and fresh tarragon.
7. Store in the refrigerator for up to 2 weeks.

**Nutrition information:** Calories per serving: 603; Carbohydrates: 1.4g; Protein: 3.5g; Fat: 66.2g; Sugar: 0g; Sodium: 497 mg; Fiber: 0.4g

# Keto Thousand Island Dressing

Serves:    10 minutes

Preparation Time: 5 minutes

Cooking Time: 2 hours

## Ingredients

- 1 cup mayonnaise
- 1 tablespoon lemon juice, freshly squeezed
- 4 tablespoons dill pickles, chopped
- 1 teaspoon Tabasco
- 1 shallot, chopped finely

## Instructions

1. Place all ingredients in the Instant Pot.
2. Add ¼ cup of water and season with salt and pepper to taste.
3. Close the lid and make sure that the vent points to "Venting."
4. Press the "Slow Cook" button and adjust the time to 2 hours.

**Nutrition information:** Calories per serving: 85; Carbohydrates: 2.3g; Protein: 1.7g; Fat: 7.8g; Sugar: 0g; Sodium: 625mg; Fiber: 1.7g

# Ketogenic Caesar Salad Dressing

Serves:   6

Preparation Time: 5 minutes

Cooking Time: 3 hours

## Ingredients

- ½ cup olive oil
- 1 tablespoon Dijon mustard
- ½ cup parmesan cheese, grated
- 2/3-ounce anchovies, chopped
- ½ lemon, juice, freshly squeezed

## Instructions

1. Place all ingredients in the Instant Pot.
2. Add ¼ cup of water and season with salt and pepper to taste.
3. Close the lid and make sure that the vent points to "Venting."
4. Press the "Slow Cook" button and adjust the time to 3 hours.

**Nutrition information:** Calories per serving:203; Carbohydrates: 1.5g; Protein: 3.4g; Fat: 20.7g; Sugar: 0g; Sodium: 296mg; Fiber: 0.6g

Made in the USA
San Bernardino, CA
28 December 2018